no disposable KIDS

Larry K. Brendtro, PhD
Arlin Ness, MSW
Martin Mitchell, EdD

Foreword by Muhammad Ali

To Alexia —
Caring for youth!
Larry Brendtro

Edited by Ruth Suli Urman and Annette Reaves
Cover design and text layout by Maria McGrorey
Production assistance by Kimberly Harris

This book contains numerous quotations by and about
troubled youth. Many of those quotations contain profanity.
In an attempt to avoid particularly offensive terms, some words
were partially replaced with hyphens. For the most part, however,
the content of those quotations remains unchanged.

ISBN 1-57035-451-0

Published and Distributed by

SOPRIS
WEST

4093 Specialty Place   •   Longmont, Colorado 80504   •   (303) 651-2829

www.sopriswest.com

159NO/EDB/9-01/13M/116

About the Authors

Larry Brendtro, Ph.D., is president of Reclaiming Youth International, a nonprofit organization networking professionals, policy leaders, and citizens concerned with troubled children. He has been a youth worker, teacher, principal, and psychologist and holds a doctorate in education and psychology from the University of Michigan. He is former president of Starr Commonwealth and taught at the University of Illinois, The Ohio State University, and Augustana College. He founded the Black Hills Seminars and co-edits the journal *Reclaiming Children and Youth*. He has trained professionals in sixteen countries, and his publications are available in several languages. His books include *Kids Who Outwit Adults*, *Reclaiming Our Prodigal Sons and Daughters*, *Reclaiming Youth at Risk*, *Positive Peer Culture*, *Re-educating Troubled Youth*, and *The Other 23 Hours*. He is a member of the U.S. Coordinating Council on Juvenile Justice and Delinquency Prevention, chaired by the attorney general. He and his wife, Janna, are the parents of two sons and a daughter, and divide their time between Traverse City, Michigan, and the Black Hills of South Dakota.

Arlin Ness, M.S.W, is president and CEO of Starr Commonwealth, which operates a range of educational and treatment programs at campuses in Michigan and Ohio. He graduated from Augustana College and holds a Master of Social Work degree from the University of Iowa. He completed advanced studies at the University of Oslo, Norway, and was a Mawby Fellow at the University of Oxford in England. He has written numerous articles on programming for troubled students and is co-author of the book, *Re-educating Troubled Youth*. He is the founding chairman of Reclaiming Youth International and has served as president of the National Association of Homes and Services for Children and as an officer on the boards of the Alliance for Children and Families and the Council of Accreditation for Human and Social Services. He frequently presents at international conferences and is currently president of the International

Association of Social Educators headquartered in Geneva, Switzerland. He and his wife, Barbara, are the parents of two adult daughters, and of two sons who passed away in childhood. They make their home on the campus of Starr Commonwealth in Albion, Michigan.

Martin Mitchell, Ed.D., is Chief Operations Officer of Starr Commonwealth. Over the past three decades, he has served as youth care worker, teacher, and program executive. He has provided legislative testimony and serves on the Public Policy Committee of the Alliance for Children and Families. His advocacy for youth has included national media including the CBS news program, *48 Hours*. Dr. Mitchell has served as president of the Michigan Association of Children's Alliances, director of the 12th World Congress of the International Association of Workers for Troubled Children and Youth, and conference director of the National Association of Homes and Services for Children. He is co-author of the books *In Whose Best Interest? One Child's Odyssey, A Nation's Responsibility and Connectedness, Continuity, Dignity and Opportunity: Principle Based Action for Kids*. Dr. Mitchell is a graduate of Olivet College and received his master's from Purdue University and his doctorate from Western Michigan University, Kalamazoo, Michigan. He and his wife, Shirlee, are the parents of three daughters and reside in Coldwater, Michigan.

About Starr Commonwealth

Founded in 1913 by Floyd Starr, Starr Commonwealth today is a private not-for-profit child and family services organization with decades of experience reaching out to people in their homes, schools, and communities. Each year, more than 7,000 young people and their families turn to Starr Commonwealth for guidance.

Starr Commonwealth's approach to working with children and families is captured in its mission statement:

> *Starr Commonwealth is dedicated to the well-being of children and families through programs and people of integrity, excellence, compassion and faith.*

Since its inception, Starr Commonwealth has changed to meet the growing needs of children and their families through strength-based programs. Never changing, though, is the philosophy that all children can succeed if given the opportunity. Starr Commonwealth embraces all people as social equals, regardless of age, nationality, gender, or ethnicity. This commitment to value and respect diversity is central to all of the organization's activities and accomplishments.

Starr Commonwealth offers programs to families in their homes, to children and staff in schools, and provides services to people in the community. There is a residential campus for youth ages 5 to 19, a specialized program for Sexually Reactive Youth, and the Montcalm School, which is a private referral residential academy designed to serve 12- to 18-year-old boys having difficulties in behavioral and academic areas. All of this is in addition to a national training resource center, an alternative education school, an adventure education program, and the new *No Disposable Kids* training package.

Table of Contents

Foreword

Muhammad Ali with Lonnie Ali

When I was young, I was privileged to be a professional boxer. The sport of boxing is no longer my field. It was a way to introduce me to the world. My most important job now is to teach people to treat each other with dignity and respect.

This book confronts the most pressing challenge facing every family, school, and community—raising respectful children in a toxic world. These pages offer hope and optimism with practical solutions for all who care about our young people. However, before the authors get to the solutions, they take us on a journey that will be enlightening, saddening, and sometimes painful. We encounter children in trouble and discover why traditional education, treatment, and discipline often fail. The authors then offer fresh approaches to turn conflicts into opportunities and create environments where all children can thrive and flourish. My wife and I have had opportunities to meet firsthand young people whose lives are being enriched and reclaimed by the methods described here. The time we spend with these young people are the greatest moments of our lives.

In simpler societies, raising children was a shared task of the whole community, as adults and youth worked in harmony and mutual respect. Today, humans are the only species in creation living out of balance. We covet our position as masters instead of servants of one another. We have forgotten that service to others is the rent we pay for our room here on earth.

Unfortunately, many who have privileges become self-indulgent and ignore those who are in need. The guardians of our laws are not always just. Schools seek to keep order by discarding the children most likely to fail in life. Courts lock away the children whom we have abused in order to "protect the public." In a world that worships power and wealth, children whose families have neither are little valued. They are considered disposable in a highly cultured and technologically advanced society.

Not only discarded children are in deep trouble. Many concerned parents are so busy making sure their children achieve success that they neglect to teach them to care for others less fortunate. Striving to make the grade, we neglect to nourish the soul. The result is that our most successful young people today mimic their materialistic elders. A survey of students entering college found that their dominant goal was to "make more money." Goals like "helping others" or "developing a meaningful philosophy of life" paled in comparison.[1] But the gold chase is a futile race. Purpose and meaning in life come from the riches of family, friends, and spiritual faith.

When I was a young man, the motto "I am the greatest" brought publicity to me and inspired young people who saw me as their hero. My boxing was just the beginning of my life. In my current career, I am trying to help all young persons find their own greatness. Very often great and beautiful things are difficult to discover. Gold is buried under layers of rock. Pearls are hidden in shells lying in the debris at the bottom of the ocean. We have to work to find them. This book challenges all of us to search for greatness in the most unlikely places, even in youth who frustrate or frighten adults.

Kids in conflict are trying to live the best they can with the hand they've been dealt. It is not always easy, since life is not equally kind to us all. We must remember to treat everyone with respect and equality. With new opportunities, many of these youth can rebuild their lives. Broken hearts can be made whole again.

I grew up in a loving family in a time when love in our nation was often hidden by racial hate. Many of my heroes were struck down in the struggle for justice. Like many youth today, we experienced tragedy, loss, and immense brutality. Yet our response to challenges make us who we are. Whatever difficulties we face, we must not lose sight of faith or let go of love. When we offer love to others, it is the net where hearts are caught like fish.

We must never look down to those who look up to us. Young people need to have some adult to turn to in the most difficult of times. Each of us is the hero some young person needs. But those youth who most deeply hunger for love often back away. They need adults who can conquer fear and rejection with love. As a onetime boxer and poet laureate of the ring, I offer a small verse about healing the human heart:

> *I am riding on my horse of hope,*
> *Holding in my hand the rein of courage.*
> *Dressed in the armor of patience,*
> *With the helmet of endurance on my head,*
> *I started out on my journey to the land of love.*[2]

When I was young, I followed for a time a teaching that disrespected others and said white people were devils. I was wrong. You cannot separate out only some of God's children to love. We are all part of the same family. In every school and neighborhood, there are children without hope, but no child is hopeless. Each was put here for a purpose. These are just children who have not yet discovered their purpose. That is our mission.

Works Cited

[1] This research is cited by David G. Meyers, professor at Hope College, Holland, Michigan. 2000. The Funds, Friends, and Faith of Happy People. *American Psychologist*, 55(1):56-67

[2] Hana Ali. 2000. *Muhammad Ali's Life Lessons Presented Through His Daughter's Eyes*. New York: Pocket Books, 56

Injustice anywhere is a threat to justice everywhere.

—Martin Luther King, Jr.[1]

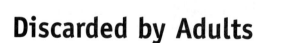

Discarded by Adults

In a world rich with material resources, millions of young people are emotionally, educationally, and spiritually adrift. Neglected by adults, they seek acceptance from other castoff peers. Fighting authority, they struggle in schools that are not structured to tap their potential. Longing for purpose, young people pursue empty substitutes in a self-centered existence. Growing up in communities that fail to respect diversity, young people are wounded by racism. Yet in spite of their troubles, these are our children, and they are all valuable to us. In a society that values children, there can be no disposable kids. At a time when many are pessimistic about the problems facing youth, this book contends that schools and communities can help all children thrive and succeed.

Over thirty years ago, we began working with challenging youth at the Starr Commonwealth, following the retirement of its founder, Floyd Starr. From its beginnings as a home and school for wayward youth, Starr now operates a network of educational and treatment programs in Michigan and Ohio. In this laboratory for positive youth development, we have learned as much from the thousands of youth who have crossed our paths as we have given to them. In this environment, youth often form alliances with their elders and become partners in their own healing.

Our school was established in 1913 with the motto, "There is no such thing as a bad boy." Four years later, Father Flanagan began Boys Town with a similar philosophy. Such pioneers were typical of the progressive educational spirit of the early twentieth century. Pioneering reformers worldwide broke free from totalitarian practices. Although predating scientific psychology, their methods were adventurous, experimental, and surprisingly effective.[2]

We were in Jerusalem at an international conference when we chose *No Disposable Kids* as the title for our book. We had toured the Children's Memorial at Yad Vashem. There, in a testament to the tragic waste of young lives, the names of children who were lost in the Holocaust are continuously read. Outside the memorial stands a statue of youth work pioneer Janusz Korczak, surrounded by children. Korczak had established orphanages and schools for Jewish street children of Warsaw. In 1942, Korczak and his staff accompanied their students to the gas chambers of Treblinka.

To a world that wasted its precious children, the Yad Vashem memorial shouts out "never again." After this moving experience, we visited a shelter for street youth in Jerusalem. There we met David who reminded us that "never again" gives way to "again and again," even in nations pledged to protect their children.

David was 18 years old and well groomed. Our first impression was that he might be a youth worker. We were surprised to learn that he was a long-term resident in this short-term facility. He stayed because no one wanted him. Hearing our American accents, David excitedly offered to be our tour guide. He showed us every corner of the antiquated three-story shelter. David explained that he had been born in Brooklyn, and was brought to Israel at age seven by his Hassidic Jewish family. His schooling had been in a Hebrew Yeshiva and he apologized for his limited English. His vocabulary, like his emotional growth, lagged at the level of a young child.

As a teen, David rebelled at the strict religious lifestyle of his family. When he began hanging out on the streets, his parents disowned him. Discarded by his family, teachers, and faith community, David searched for a purpose to his life. He invited us into his small room, eager to display a drawer of religious tracts he had collected from various street ministries. He inquired about the cost of a plane ticket to America, saying he wanted to return to the land of his birth. Much too soon, it was time for us to leave. Like a small, discouraged boy, David asked, "Will this will be the last time I will ever talk with you?"

As we departed, we were reminded of the "Circle of Courage" principles that guide our work: Children develop courage through *belonging, mastery, independence, and generosity.* In our short time with David, we saw his hunger to belong, to master, to be independent, and to be generous in spirit. But David was discouraged. His circle had been broken.

While David's background is unique, discarded kids everywhere are much the same. Some seek substitute belongings through chemicals, cults, or gangs. Many middle class children roam in packs as mall orphans. Children of privilege may be bloated with possessions but starving in loveless mansions. Schools often have the least tolerance for students with the greatest needs.

It is no puzzle what youth like David need. For a century, the great masters in education and youth work have shown how to build courage in discouraged children. Today, practical, research-validated methods are available for prevention. We also know how to reclaim many of our most difficult youth.

Policy leaders need positive answers to pressing problems, and those who are in face-to-face contact with challenging youth are hungry for fresh strategies.

Ben Carson was a student at risk from an impoverished African American community. Today he is one of the world's leading pediatric neurosurgeons. Speaking of the challenges of working with difficult children, he says: "Every young person we keep from going down the path of self-destruction is one less person from whom we have to protect ourselves and our families, one less person we have to pay for in the penal or welfare system, and one more productive member of society who may come up with the cure for cancer or AIDS. We cannot afford to throw them away."[3]

We have introduced each chapter in *No Disposable Kids* with the unfolding story of a young boy who grew up in a highly troubled environment. But whether children experience adversity or advantage, they have the same basic needs. All must find belonging, master their world, gain responsible independence, and be of value to others. Meeting these needs is a birthright for every child. When we permit any child to grow up in a hostile environment, all of our children are in danger.

Works Cited

[1] These words are prominently inscribed at the Martin Luther King Memorial in Atlanta, Georgia.

[2] Bridgeland. 1971.

[3] Ben Carson. 2000. Founder's Day speech. Starr Commonwealth, Albion, Michigan, October 1, 2000. Ben Carson, MD, is a former youth at risk and is now director of Pediatric Neurosurgery at Johns Hopkins in Baltimore, Maryland.

Rebel With a Cause

*Violence—whatever else it may mean—
is the ultimate means of communicating
the absence of love.*

—James Gilligan[1]

*The day began like any other. As children left their homes for
school, parents bid them goodbye. Most families were secure in
the satisfaction that their youngsters were enrolled in a safe
school, protected from the violence of less privileged neighborhoods. Students entered their school building[1] where laughter
echoed through the halls. Nobody was aware that a troubled boy
and his alter ego would soon unleash a deadly inferno. Before
the day was out, many died and hundreds more were scarred for
the rest of their lives.*

*The most destructive school violence in history occurred on
December 1, 1958, at Our Lady of Angels elementary school in*

Chicago. Ninety-two students and three teachers died in a fire thought to be intentionally set by a student.[2]

Our Lady of Angels school was located five miles west of the downtown Chicago Loop. This was a well-kept, tree-lined neighborhood in one of the leading Catholic parishes in Chicago. The residents of this primarily Italian community took great pride in their parochial school.

The fire began in a barrel of trash beneath the basement stairs. The stairwell soon became a chimney, shooting flames through the building. Teachers led younger children from the lower floors to safety. Many older students were trapped on the upper levels by intense heat and smoke that filled the hallways. Barricaded in their classrooms, they waited to be evacuated by ladders.

The fire quickly drew a large crowd of horrified onlookers including parents of children trapped in the building. The fire trucks arrived to find an iron fence blocking access to the school. Some who escaped by jumping from the upper story rooms were seriously injured. Nearly 200 were able to get out on ladders. But many never got out. Students and teachers died together, praying for rescue.

The Chicago American *published a memorial edition four days after the fire. The front page was covered with school photos of many of the victims. This display of happy faces looked like a grade school graduating class. To friends and relatives, these victims would remain children forever.*

For months, Chicago media covered the fire story. Rumors ran rampant. Everyone speculated about the cause of the disaster. Some blamed the building design or the fire department's response speed. Controversy swirled around all connected with the school, from the bishop to the building's janitor. Interrogators grilled boys suspected of smoking cigarettes in the basement. Authorities gathered statements from every student and school employee. In the end, all leads turned cold.

For years, newspapers ran features on the anniversary of the disaster. Many citizens remembered where they were when they heard of the second great Chicago fire. Gradually the story faded from the memory of all except those personally touched by this tragedy.

Privately, many authorities were convinced that the Angels fire was purposely set, probably by a student. Crime profilers knew that most children who set fires were boys. The blaze began in the basement where the boys' bathroom was located. Every male student had easy access to that area of the building.

Meanwhile, the mother of one student who had survived the fire harbored her own suspicions. Her son Tony was often playing with matches, and he had set other small fires in the neighborhood. Her greatest fear was that he might have started this one, too.

Tony's mother allegedly had been raped by her own stepfather. At the age of 15, she gave birth to her son in a home for unwed mothers. She was supposed to give her child up for adoption. But when the time came to sign the papers, she refused to let anybody take her child away. Though lacking mature parenting skills, this friendless girl set out for distant Chicago with her infant son.

Little is known of Tony's early childhood, although the young mother lived for a time with relatives in Chicago. Just what happened to Tony in his chaotic childhood is not certain. But the first sign that something terribly wrong had happened to him came at age five: Tony began setting fires.

For a half century, fire setting by children has been linked to sexual abuse.[3] Victimized children feel powerless and often act out in ways that replay their trauma. They may destroy possessions, mutilate themselves, hurt pets, and light fires. Boys who have been prematurely sexualized can be aroused by irrelevant stimulation such as physical punishment, hearing sirens, or watching fires.[4] Although sexual abuse was never documented in Tony's records, it would explain his fire setting.

Tony's emotional problems spilled over to school and peer relationships. This small, chubby, blonde boy with thick glasses was ridiculed and bullied by peers. At Angels school, Sister Carolan taught Tony religion and counseled him. She described him as a boy starving for a male role model. He was hungry for interaction with the two priests assigned to the school. Sister Carolan saw him as a practical joker who acted up for attention but meant no harm. He was always remorseful when he had done something wrong.

Other teachers were not so kind in their assessment. Although Tony was intelligent, he needed close supervision. He restlessly roamed through the school. His teacher sent other students to locate him and escort him back to class. In contemporary terms, his behavior might qualify as attention deficit disorder. Such students require constant correction and can become embroiled in conflict with authorities. What starts as inattention escalates to rebellion.

Tony's mother was well aware of his problems. For years she had tried her best to protect him from frustrated teachers and unfriendly peers. Since leaving home at 15, Tony was all the family she had, and the two of them stood against the world. Authorities wanted to take him away when he was an infant— what if they learned of his problems now? She couldn't risk losing her son. She would watch him more closely to make sure that he didn't get into trouble. Perhaps if Tony had a father. . . .

Area fire investigators kept a roster of students enrolled in Our Lady of Angels school at the time of the fire. In any other case when arson was suspected, they cross-checked the names of juvenile suspects against this roster. Police were unaware that shortly after the Angels fire, a troubled fifth-grade boy moved from the parish to the suburb of Cicero. His single mother had married and Tony now had a stepfather. He also gained a new name but retained his old ways. For three years, authorities were unable to connect this boy to the fire that killed 92 students and three teachers.

Pathways to Trouble

Early in the path toward delinquency there is a break down in the connections to home, school, and family.

—Alfred Kazdin[5]

All social learning begins in the family environment. Being reared by caring adults is essential to the development of character and conscience. Good parenting requires providing both affection and discipline. Secure in love and limits, children are prepared to extend their positive relationships to school, peers, and the community. When these bonds are broken, youth are on a pathway to trouble.

A wide variety of pressures on the modern family can disrupt parenting. These include a hurried lifestyle, work pressures, poverty, wealth, divorce, illness, disability, criminality, alcoholism, and abuse. Some children who have difficult temperaments can add stress to their family's lives. Adults who are extremely stressed or who lack parenting skills do not form the secure bonds necessary to teach their children social competence and self-control. Children who experience inconsistent or hostile parenting develop undisciplined behavior marked by power struggles and coercive interactions. Difficult temperaments and family disruptions also interfere with the development of secure attachments. Children with trusting bonds to parents seldom develop a pattern of serious antisocial behavior.[6]

Positive bonds to school foster prosocial growth. Students who are weakly attached to their families are particularly dependent on supportive teachers. School mastery is a powerful antidote to antisocial behavior. However, when youth bring their home problems to school, teachers may not be skilled at managing these challenging children. Inadvertently, they can recreate the conflict and stress of the child's earlier relationships.

Schools depend heavily on punishment and exclusion to manage behavior. Punitive "get tough" or avoidant "kick out" strategies are feel-good responses. In the short term, they lessen immediate adult stress or settle the school environment. However, adults who become counter-aggressive or rejecting further rupture a youth's social bond and thus reinforce antisocial behavior. When students reject discipline, however, it prevents them from bonding to their school.

School failure propels youth toward antisocial peers. Even higher status "good kids" can contribute to creating environments where lower status students become scapegoats. Students in conflict with adults and rejected by positive peers adopt "bad kid" identities. Academic failure is commonplace and self-esteem plummets. To satisfy their powerful need to belong, by grades four or five youth actively recruit friendships with other antisocial students, forming little gangs of rule breakers and bullies. Martin Gold calls this "school-induced delinquency."

As antisocial students disengage academically, they become powerfully dependent on peers who support one another in their hatred of school and teachers. In general, positive peer bonds foster prosocial growth, and bonding to peers is usually a healthy process. Even among youth who are troublemakers, 90 percent affirm positive values and desire positive friends even though the peer group encourages defiance and rebellion. Bonding to delinquent peers can enhance a youth's self-esteem. In contrast, children who are loners, cut off from both adults and peers, show pervasive insecurity and depression.

Children who are weakly bonded to family or school find substitute belonging by joining other alienated peers. This negative subculture indoctrinates them into ever more risky behavior, including sexual precocity, delinquency, and substance abuse. Antisocial friendships often begin at school and move to the street as youth gain more independence from authority. Many are not accountable to responsible adults. Immersed in drug or delinquent subcultures, they learn values and skills from peers and perhaps from exploitative drug-involved or criminal adults.

As youth associate with negative peers, antisocial values, thinking, and behavior are reinforced. Ratcheting up the severity of punishment has little effect on the most troubled youth since they either do not think ahead or believe they will escape detection and in some cases don't care if they are caught.

Troubled youth often are frightening or repugnant to adults unable to understand or manage them. Thus, students who don't readily comply with expectations of those in authority are usually given less rather than more support. Faith communities often actively shun children who could benefit from church youth groups. Untrained adults who are insecure in their ability to work with these youth are highly motivated to get rid of them. Unlike children with other handicaps, troubled kids are blamed for their disability even though they have serious emotional and behavioral problems. They also are given disparaging labels such as disrespectful, disobedient, troublemakers, losers, criminals, predators, or perpetrators. Even psychiatric labels become pejorative: emotionally disturbed, behaviorally disordered, conduct disordered, oppositional defiant disordered, and sociopathic. Viewed this way, positive traits are obscured and these youth evoke little empathy from their elders.

Cultures of Disrespect

Communities of civility do not mass-produce disrespectful children. Positive social control comes from social bonds between people who care for one another. A person who disrespects others is often one who has not been treated with dignity. Most violence begins as a private affair in homes where children and adults do not develop respectful relationships. Disrespect can extend to peer groups, school, and the streets. Even schools of privilege often are ruled by cliques of popular kids who lord it over lower status peers. Violence can erupt from this process of exclusion.

In a supreme irony, disrespectful methods may be used in an attempt to teach respect. Hoping to create an orderly environment, a New York school empowered a student court to administer punishments. The court required students who violated rules to wear bright pink t-shirts imprinted with "Student Offender." Said a school official, "Many of these [young people] were fighting, bullying, or verbally abusing other people or causing trouble on the bus. We are trying to say that violence isn't an option." The student editor of the school newspaper called the court "a student hate committee" because it inflicted shame and humiliation. Opponents claimed public shaming legitimized harassment, as students hurled taunts, some of a sexual nature, at classmates dressed in pink. This punishment was deeply humiliating to some students. Others wore the shirts as badges of honor, bolstering their defiance.[7]

Shaming students into submission is a core practice in adult-dominance models of education. An Australian youth told us the phrase they hate most is "You are a no-hoper." Chinese schools are currently attempting to curtail this tradition since ridicule phrases have long been used to intimidate trembling charges. A survey of 20,000 Chinese students and teachers came up with 5,000 demeaning phrases. The worst 40 phrases that are now officially forbidden include these examples:[8]

> "Whoever teaches you has the worst luck."
> "You are a round post with two ears. Get out!"
> "If I were you, I would not continue to live. You are hopeless."

Even students who act in outrageous ways desperately desire respect. Many adults find it difficult to act respectfully toward youth whose behavior invites disrespect. In some settings, adults and youth alike treat one another with disrespect and antagonism. This is not just a problem among disadvantaged students:

> A 14-year-old freshman at McLean High School in wealthy Fairfax County (VA) said, "I was talking to one of my friends and the teacher said something like 'shut up' and it pissed me off so I said, 'Go to

hell, [expletive] you.'" Gisela, a junior at McLean, said, "I explained why I was late to my teacher and she started going off on me about what I needed to do to get to school on time. I just freaked out and called her the b- word…. I got Saturday detention but I don't regret it. She deserved to be called that."[9]

In a positive community, persons who act disrespectfully suffer serious social consequences. If social bonds are strong, even mild criticism can produce shame and motivate corrective action.[10] But hostile and disrespectful criticism causes angry pride and defiance.[11] In a respectful group, members confront the behavior while accepting the person. In a climate of disrespect, individuals feel violated.[12] In the language of the street, this is being "dissed," a provocation to violence.

Authority figures enhance their legitimacy by showing respect. The community policing movement best demonstrates this. In the past, many urban police operated with their own street code of zero-tolerance for disrespect. A law enforcement expert notes, "There is no written law against 'contempt of cop,' of course, but it is perhaps the most consistently enforced de facto law in the country…. Disrespect toward police powerfully increases the odds of being arrested."[13] Troubled kids are only too willing to violate this code. In Boston, police and youth had the same negative views of one another. Once they had opportunities for positive interaction, the past patterns of mutual disrespect declined, as did street crime.

Cultures of disrespect spark aggression. Arnold Goldstein observes that in Western societies, children are surrounded by aggression in home, school, and community. Ninety percent of families in the United States make occasional or frequent use of physical punishment. Schools can become staging grounds for the lessons of "Aggression 101."[14] Finally, the media, radio, movies, video games, and television provide an almost unremitting diet of violence. Research suggests that this nonstop overdosing on violence has three effects: (1) It directly increases aggressive acts; (2) It fosters a victim mentality with increased

Art by Denisha, age 17

fearfulness and mistrust; and (3) It desensitizes bystanders who become callous to aggressive acts they observe.

Permissiveness or tolerance for hostile acts further reinforces a climate of disrespect. This contradicts a popular notion in psychology that catharsis—allowing a person to "vent" hostility—will drain off aggression.[15] All evidence is to the contrary. Hurting or disrespectful behavior is a recipe for aggression as numerous studies show that violent actions or words, or even viewing violence, all increase aggressive behavior. Of course, positive catharsis—talking things out, creative expression, exercise, or even altruism—can reduce stress and aggression.[16]

Both adults and children need to learn to solve problems without resorting to hostility and conflict. An attorney described attempts to discipline his strong-willed 12-year-old son, Ronnie. The father found a CD in Ronnie's dresser drawer and was shocked that it had rap lyrics about raping mothers. He confronted his son, reminding him that the CD player was a gift, and now he was playing music that was disrespectful to his own mother. Instead of showing regret or humility, Ronnie became angry that his father had searched his bedroom. The father also became furious: "Before I knew it, I had hurled the CD player onto the floor, bashing it into smithereens. Ronnie tried to escape by taking off on his bike. I ordered him to stop but he kept going. I wasn't going to tolerate disrespect so I took after him in my SUV. When I saw him with his friends, I drove up and told him we could finish our discussion in front of his friends or back at home." After it was over, the father felt terrible and his son was not speaking to him. "I am a lawyer and I help people resolve conflicts every day. How could I lose it like that? He used to look up to me; he doesn't even want to be around me now."

Most serious school conflicts begin with low-level aggression that escalates out of control. Since it is easier to solve small problems, this suggests a strategy of "catch it low to prevent it high."[17] Goldstein contends that zero-tolerance for aggression is a valid principle. But zero-tolerance has nothing to do with inflicting punishment or giving up on difficult children. Such approaches are likely to increase aggression.

Cycles of Hostility

When normal needs are frustrated, problem behavior results. Love deprivation during childhood and adolescence is a significant cause of antisocial behavior.[18] Ashley Montague said, "Take almost any violent individual and inquire into his history as a child and it can be predicted with confidence that he will be discovered to have had a lack love childhood, to have suffered a failure of tender loving care. Those delinquents who are the most dangerous are closely associated with the classic antisocial psychopath."[19] Behind the behavior of people who hate and hurt others without guilt are young people who, instead of feeling love and encouragement, experienced threat, rejection, deprivation, and mistreatment from adults.[20]

In a typical year, three million children in the United States enter the child welfare system because of allegations of neglect or abuse. A similar number come into contact with the juvenile justice system. Research by the Child Welfare League of America shows that these are often the same adolescents. Children who experience neglect or abuse are 67 times more likely to engage in delinquent acts before their teen years.[21]

Mistreated children begin as powerless victims of neglect, brutalization, and violent subjugation. Some remain helpless victims for life. Others reach a point where they decide to reject their victim status and fight back. They have been "violentized," transformed from victim into victimizer. This process actually can give a new sense of defiant pride.[22] Psychologist Aaron Kipnis describes the point when he decided to no longer take abuse from his stepfather, Zombie:

> That morning, yanked straight from sleep into a violent assault, I suddenly reached a boiling point. Having grown stronger and more confident about my fighting ability, I hit back, swift and hard. Zombie was stunned. He instantly became frenzied. His face turned red. He began bellowing at me and punching me in earnest. I weighed about 100 pounds and he weighed over 200, so there was clearly no chance of my winning the fight. But I didn't care. I felt he had to learn that, from now on, there would be a price to pay for hitting me.... Having caused a grown man to back down from a violent attack, I felt a new sense of power.[23]

Kipnis was slightly built and not tied to a gang so he was always at risk of confrontations from older boys. He decided to compensate for his size by reacting violently to the slightest gesture of disrespect and created an aura of safety: "I tried to project a 'don't f--- with me anytime, anywhere' attitude. It prevented most assaults from occurring."[24]

Not all youth can turn victimization into violence. Aggression is not a preferred strategy for mild-mannered and easily intimidated youth. Thus, the ranks of bullies and delinquents contain more boys than girls and more gutsy extroverts than placid introverts. Aggression is better matched to fearless rather than anxious personalities and to people who crave excitement and are impervious to pain. All of these personal characteristics are correlated with *Disruptive Behavior Disorders*, a catchall term for the psychiatric diagnoses of Attention Deficit Hyperactivity Disorder, Oppositional Defiant Disorder, and Conduct Disorder.

Youth pioneers have described similar behavior in wild kids for a century, but without belittling labels. Jane Addams, who sparked the juvenile court movement, saw troubled youth mainly in terms of their strengths. She observed that delinquents have a greater spirit of adventure than other youth. In colonial America, such boys sailed out to sea to find thrills. Without such opportunities, they create delinquent excitement on the streets through theft, vandalism, and gang fights. We suspect that if Jane Addams were compelled to assign a mental health diagnosis to troubled adolescents, she might have used upbeat labels like "Bravado Behavior Disorder" or "Spirit of Youth Syndrome."

Even shy children from stable families can be driven to violence. When the pain of ridicule or rejection becomes too great, such youth can come to a point where life almost means nothing to them anyway, which makes them very powerful. In the end, it only takes the stroke of a match or a finger on a trigger to transform a victim into a dangerous victimizer. Behind the most dramatic case of school violence, one often finds a history of peer victimization.

Ridicule and Bullying

Tanya approached her classroom in silent terror, preparing to pass by a group of boys near the water fountain. She tried to ignore them as they made various animal sounds and started a mock dispute about whether she smelled more like a pig or a cow. Looking on were two girls who earlier that morning on the bus had been making fun of Tanya's clothing. Now, they joined the boys in gales of laughter. The teacher came to the hall to check on the commotion, but Tanya quickly said, "It's OK,

they're not bothering me; we're just having fun."
Past incidents had taught her that complaining only
invited more abuse. Later she explained, "My
mother said I should just say, 'Sticks and stones
may break my bones but words will never hurt me.'
But this is worse than sticks and stones."

Each day, hundreds of thousands of students like Tanya are
ridiculed and bullied by their peers. When verbal aggression
escalates into physical violence, most schools respond decisive-
ly. However, the vast majority of school bullying is not overt
violence but covert psychological warfare. It comes in the form
of social ridicule, psychological intimidation, and group rejection. As the example suggests, girls are doubly vulnerable to
sexist harassment by miseducated boys.[25]

Teasing can be innocent fun and a bond of friendship. But when
teasing mutates into ridicule, it is no longer play. Neither is
ridicule a natural social learning experience preparing children
to better cope with a rough and tumble world. *Ridicule is a
powerful social ritual designed to demean certain individuals
and set them apart from others*. Those so stigmatized become
what anthropologists call "polluted persons." This devalued status gives license for members of the in-group to abuse the outcasts without fear of punishment.

Ridicule is psychological bullying. It can include mocking,
insults, and "humor" designed to make the person an object of
scorn or ridicule. Among girls, spreading rumors and exclusion
from the group are common bullying behaviors.

Girls in a middle school reported to their parents
that they had heard a rumor that Lyla, an unpopu-
lar girl in special education, had threatened to
bring a gun to school to shoot other students.
Since it was the weekend, appropriately concerned
parents contacted the police. Their investigation
showed that no such threat was ever made, but that
two other girls thought it would be fun to spread
this nasty rumor about Lyla.

Insults can target a person's appearance, personality, family, race, gender, or values. Ridicule doesn't even require words since dirty looks and gestures will accomplish the same ends. All of these cross the line from playful teasing to disrespect and demean a person.

Even in schools with abundant resources, 25 percent of children report they are afraid of bullies. Most children quickly discover that they cannot rely on teachers to protect them from these attacks. In fact, much bullying behavior occurs in or around school but outside the immediate surveillance of teachers. Victims of bullying try to navigate through the school with a mental map of unsafe zones such as bathrooms, the playground, and along the route to and from school. Fearful children who try to keep close to teachers only risk peer ridicule as teacher's pet.

Subtle bullying can occur in classrooms since some forms of ridicule are calculated to avoid detection, such as when peers roll their eyes in derision or participate in the social banishment of a fellow student. Sometimes teachers spot these behaviors but choose to ignore them in the hope that children will learn to handle these problems independently. In 400 hours of video-documented episodes of bullying at school, teachers noticed and intervened in only one out of every 25 episodes.[26]

Serious research on school bullying began a quarter century ago in Scandinavian schools with the pioneering work of Dan Olweus of Norway.[27] The fledgling "science of bullying" has established important facts about the profiles of bullies and victims. Typically, less than ten percent of students are active bullies, and a similar number are perpetual victims. The most powerful role in the drama is played by the audience. Some become the cheering section for bullies, while a silent majority of bystanders enable bullying by their silence. Programs to bully-proof schools can reduce a whole range of antisocial behaviors and school discipline problems. Successful programs change the climate and values of schools by mobilizing adults and students in an alliance to create a powerful caring environment.

Researchers who began studying school bullying in the United States were startled to find that peer victimization occurs at much higher rates than in Europe. This climate of peer violence is found in rural as well as urban schools. Yet in spite of a body of knowledge about preventing bullying, schools in the United States vacillate between ignoring bullies or harshly punishing or excluding them. Such practices haven't changed school climates, and there is always an understudy waiting to assume the role of head troublemaker if negative students are sent off to special settings.

Initially, most researchers assumed that physical aggression was the most damaging form of bullying behavior. School bullying research shows that teasing is the most prevalent type of bullying.[28] This verbal ridicule and harassment is often as devastating as periodic physical abuse by peers. The long-term effects of ridicule, insult, and rejection are on a par with physical abuse.[29]

Ridicule is a direct attack on a child's sense of self-worth. If it persists, it can have life-altering effects. Experiencing ridicule evokes strong negative emotions of shame, anxiety, and fear. Most children become angry at their mistreatment but feel helpless to stop it. Some conclude that they are worthless individuals who deserve rejection. Instead of recognizing that others are treating them badly, they see themselves as bad and shameful people. When continual ridicule overwhelms a child's ability to hope and cope, a crisis ensues. That person may become depressed and self-destructive or, in isolated circumstances, strike out at others. In many dramatic cases of school violence, individuals who see themselves as victims of ridicule acquire weapons or antisocial allies and take vengeance on their victimizers.

Bullies pummel the self-esteem of victims to make themselves feel powerful. They build a counterfeit self-esteem by putting others down. Research suggests that many bullies have lots of confidence, enjoy dominating others, and are comfortable with aggression. They feel little empathy for their victims. Usually, they have a conscience, but they justify their behavior with thinking errors. They give demeaning labels to victims ("he's a wimp"), minimize the hurting impact of their own behavior ("we were just kidding"), and blame the victim ("he had it coming"). With this twisted thinking, a student can silence the voice of conscience.[30]

While "bullying" is a term with male overtones, girls can also be proficient bullies. Mary Pipher notes that traditional role expectations restrict aggression by girls who then rely on spite and character assassination. They mock peers who don't have the right clothes or fail to conform to cultural stereotypes about femininity. A girl might punish a peer by calling her on the phone to tell her there is going to be a party but she is not invited. They scapegoat other girls for failing to achieve the same impossible goals they are unable to achieve. Some even pick on a girl who seems happy in order to make her life as miserable as theirs.[31]

Many boys might be described as "recreational bullies" whose behavior is a way to gain macho status. When bullying is no longer seen as funny or cool, these youths lose their power. A positive peer culture transforms many former bullies into positive leaders who use their strength to befriend and protect those who are vulnerable. A student from Norway recalled an experience in elementary school when a new pupil was enrolled in her classroom. Her teacher gave the biggest boy in the room a badge that said, "Don't bully my friend," and assigned him as host to the new pupil.

The most potent single cause of bullying is a negative peer group climate. The rank and file doesn't speak up when someone is being hurt. When challenged by peers, most bullies desist. Still, a small minority of bullies continues to pose problems even in caring schools. Their hostility springs from a deep well. John Hoover calls them "bull-vics" because they have been severely victimized themselves and now displace their anger on others. They need targeted interventions in order to break from patterns of antisocial thinking, feelings, and behavior. In Norwegian schools, the most potent discipline is what educators call "very serious conversations." Interventions with such students need to make them uncomfortable with hurting others. This involves developing empathy for victims and removing the payoff for bullying.

When students don't feel socially and/or physically safe, the school climate is rife with rankling and ridicule. In such environments, even ordinary students are capable of extraordinary meanness. Cliques are formed with membership dictated by race, style of clothing, athletic prowess, or other superficial traits that Polly Nichols calls "lookism."[32] Joining these alliances gives students a sense of superiority and belonging at the expense of those who are banished.

All adults can help stop harassment, although they certainly cannot become ridicule police. Only when the climate of the youth subculture challenges violence will real change be possible. Although students who observe bullying may feel some empathy for the victim, they seldom step forward to defend this peer lest they also become targets. This failure to help is particularly tragic since a student who knows he or she has at least one friend can better endure the adversity of rejection.

Changing school climates requires more than recruiting a few brave children who will be buddies with rejected students. Indeed, bullying behavior will persist unless it becomes unacceptable to the silent majority. Without intervention, half of elementary school-age bullies will go on to adult criminal behavior. Schools that address this problem can make significant reductions in immediate and long-term antisocial behavior.

A difficult challenge in anti-bullying programs is getting educators to understand the negative effects bullying has on all students.[33] Jim Longhurst found that some teachers believed that bullying is a natural part of growing up and isn't such a big deal. Even worse is the universal notion that students with inappropriate social skills actually deserve to be bullied or may benefit from ridicule, shunning, and intimidation. Moreover, teachers cannot effectively deal with bullying if they unwittingly or intentionally employ bullying tactics in classroom management. Schools that tolerate ridicule and bullying foster disrespectful climates that damage all students.

Negative Peer Cultures

"The newspapers have recorded, day after day, numbers of intolerable, and occasionally even fatal outrages upon unoffending citizens, especially on women and children, committed by gangs of young roughs, armed with belts, bludgeons, and at times with pistols." This account is from London of 1898.[34] In the same era, Jane Addams described almost daily shootings by Chicago youth who had easy access to firearms.[35] Gangs, ethnic conflict, and gun violence are not a recent phenomenon. They are common whenever youth groups operate beyond the influence of positive adults. Addams cited a wide variety of cases to show that most problem behaviors of youth are generated among peers pumped by group excitement.

In antisocial groups, negative behavior is maintained because youth believe their peers value delinquency more than they do. Youth fear scorn or violence if they do not act tough. They unwittingly egg one another on in outrageous behavior to impress peers.[36] For example, one youth exclaimed "Oh, shoot!" in front of peers and then quickly corrected himself to "Oh, shit!" in order to appear appropriately rough.

Schools and youth institutions often serve as staging areas for antisocial youth subcultures.[37] Negative peers are potentially destructive in any setting. Hostile cliques are commonplace in many schools. One of the most interesting accounts of negative youth subcultures came from the research of Howard Polsky. For eight months he lived as a "participant observer" with a group of aggressive youths in a highly respected residential school. Once he gained the trust of the youths, he gained entrance into a world that is otherwise hidden from adult surveillance.

A powerful hidden hierarchy among students undermined educational and treatment goals. At the top of the pecking order were those adolescents most able to intimidate peers, either physically or psychologically. At the bottom were weak or passive students who were targets of the aggression. In the middle were the majority of status-hungry students who would do almost anything to keep in good graces with the negative leaders. Adults thought they were running a progressive, well-staffed program; in reality, this was a little totalitarian society ruled by peer violence and intimidation.

When a new student was enrolled, established members would "rank" this person by attributing real or imagined weaknesses. In this culture of pseudo-masculine toughness, boys who chose not to fight back were labeled, for example, "queers" and acquired permanent scapegoat status. For example, students harassed a timid boy, Chuck, by accusing him of having sex with a dog. Unable to defend against their spectacular allegations, Chuck became the constant butt of escalating hateful humor.

Scapegoating was not isolated but became "the warp and woof of the social structure." Most scapegoats meekly accepted their roles, so few repercussions were felt throughout the school. Adults were ignorant of this victimization or chose to ignore it. Some were actually seduced into the bullying process by making disparaging remarks about low-status members and recognizing bullies for their leadership. In this culture of intimidation, many poorly trained teachers and administrative workers became victims of a kind of reverse behavior modification, in which their actions were shaped by the aggressive youths. Such staff tried to show their own toughness with intimidating language and demeanor, thereby modeling bullying behavior.

People do things as part of a group that they never would do as individuals. Acting in groups with others, individual responsibility is diluted. *USA Today* reported how a troubled youngster on a Southwest Airlines flight was apparently killed by fellow passengers. The youth was trying to get into the cockpit to fly the plane and attempted to open an exit door. Several male passengers reportedly pummeled, stomped, and choked him to death in the aisle. Many more watched this happen; none were held responsible.[38]

Group behavior is contagious and members are easily lured into attacking a person who is disliked or devalued. In the book, *Ordinary People and Extraordinary Evil*, Fred Katz studied how otherwise respectable people get ensnared in atrocities like the Holocaust or military massacres of civilians.[39] These actions contradict the values of individuals who become swept up in group-think mentality.

Youth are highly vulnerable to group-think and most "antisocial" behavior occurs in a social group. Katz suggests we teach adolescents to bail out of the group at the first sign of evil. Otherwise group seduction can lead to disastrous consequences. Most individuals lack the courage to resist violence coaching from charismatic or intimidating peers. Katz concluded that all of us are capable of extraordinary evil if we yield personal morality to the group. Such was the case with four youths who took the life of an elderly man.

Lives Interrupted

Mark, Chad, Joshua, and James were hanging out at a bowling alley in Grand Rapids, Michigan. They spotted an elderly African American bowler, 66-year-old Willie Jones, who had a wallet stuffed with money. Beginning with the motive of theft, they abducted him from the bowling alley, beat him severely, and then threw him in the trunk of their car. As they drove around, they stopped to show Willie to some friends, like captured prey. Then they drove to a nearby wooded area where Willie was stabbed repeatedly with a scissors and then left to die in the woods. All four boys were convicted of murder. Each had been in the juvenile system for several years.

When we read of this savage crime, we were shocked to discover that two of the youths were former students at the Starr Commonwealth. How could these four young men come together to destroy another human and ruin their own lives in a senseless night of group terror? A dozen years earlier they were eager first-graders and now they will spend their lives locked up in prison. As seen from their profiles, the boys followed separate pathways to their common catastrophe.[40] The participants played very different roles; some dominated and others were easily misled.

Mark had a long history of serious violence. When he started school, he would get on the school bus and pick on other kids. By second grade, Mark was assaulting other students with rocks, baseball bats, and a knife. Nobody ever figured out what caused Mark's rage, but his parents were required to take substance abuse classes. When Mark was 13 and the courts gave his grandmother temporary custody, he was described as mean and angry. He was charged with assault with a knife, felonious assault, and larceny. Mark spent time in detention, but never received intensive treatment. At age 16, he was involved in drug offenses and driving a stolen car. He threatened a teacher in school and went looking for a gun to carry out his threats. When living with his grandmother, Mark ran away from home. When she tracked him down and made him return to school, he threatened to kill her. She was at her wit's end. Mark told her that he had stolen a car and dumped it in the river. When she asked him why, he just laughed and laughed. When she heard of the killing, she feared Mark was involved.

Chad at age five was a needy child looking for love. There were allegations of neglect and abuse, and he had seen the imprisonment and death of his father. He was often teased "like father, like son." His grandmother reported that by age ten, Chad seemed to lack a conscience. He had no sense of purpose, didn't care if he got caught, grounded, or suspended from school. He would look at her, pick up her purse, and walk out of the house with it. He was assigned court ordered community service and counseling, but he skipped sessions, destroyed property, and shot out windows. In middle school, he stole a teacher's car. He was held five times in the county juvenile facility, and he ran away from foster home placements. He was placed in a Colorado facility but that program was shut down after allegations of sexual misconduct by staff. His grandmother said, "He was given a lot of opportunities by the authorities but there was also a lot of emotional killing done to Chad before he ever got to that bowling alley. He got set on this road, and I don't know if there is any way to turn him back."

Joshua was one of the boys who had once been enrolled at Starr Commonwealth. He had many problems but also made periodic progress when given stable environments. However, Joshua was derailed by rejection from his mother. Joshua had almost no contact with his father, whose whereabouts were unknown. At age ten, he got into trouble for stealing construction machinery; both he and his brother had various burglary charges. Some charges were apparently committed under coercion by adults. At age 13, he brought a gun to middle school and was placed in a court program for at-risk offenders. He flourished and was eligible to return home, but his mother said it wasn't convenient to have him. After foster placements failed, he was sent to Starr Commonwealth when he was 15. He was upset at the lack of visits from his mother. A black woman befriended Joshua and took him into her home; he called her mom. She reports that he was really trying to become a better person but didn't have the right friends. News of his arrest for killing an elderly black man sickened her. "For him to do that, to pick on a crippled old black man and do that, I just couldn't fathom it. It was like he did that to my family."

James had also been enrolled at Starr. He had a long history of offenses, including being caught with a gun and a stolen vehicle. His mother was on public assistance and his father had spent time in jail. He was involved in destruction of property, shoplifting, and possession of marijuana. His mother allegedly kicked him out of her home. James then entered a counseling program for homeless youth and was given independent living status. He was not keeping required contact with his probation officer at the time of the killing. One of the other boys used James's high school class ring to inflict more damage on Mr. Jones. James couldn't bear to watch or listen when Mr. Jones was taken to a remote wooded area, beaten, stabbed, and left for dead. "I pray that God will forgive me for being such a coward," James told police.

The experience of Joshua and James demonstrates that even adolescents who know what is right can be caught up in antisocial group behavior and lack the strength to buck group influence. This problem is not just with serious delinquents, it is a concern shared by most parents who recognize the awesome power of peer influence.

Dark Thinking

A third-grader became wild and disrespectful and was removed from class almost daily. After several weeks, the staff learned that she and older siblings were living on a deserted farm where their mother had abandoned them. Fearful of being separated, the children told no one and continued riding the bus to school each day.

An outgoing teen suddenly became morose and withdrawn. A scrape with police led to probation. In opening up about his life to his juvenile officer, he felt he was betrayed. "That's when I found out you couldn't trust anyone. So from being friendly with everyone I met, I started turning everyone off and didn't speak to anyone."[41]

Often it is difficult to understand problems without knowing the distressed thoughts and feelings that trigger these behaviors. Polly Nichols calls this "dark thinking."[42] Even seemingly "senseless" acts usually make sense if we understand the private logic and motives of the individual. To understand is not to excuse the behavior, but to be better able to prevent and change it.

Our most important source of information about behavior is careful observation. But observing surface behavior may leave us puzzled about its underlying purpose. The same problem springs from various causes—both punitive and permissive child rearing can lead to aggression. A given "cause" can also produce very different effects in children—abuse leads some to withdraw and others to attack. What you see is not always what you get. Children as young as three can act in ways calculated to deceive and confuse adults. Thus, changing problem behavior often requires discovering its purpose. One way of doing this is to analyze the child's prior events and conditions and his or her consequences of behavior. Federal law mandates such assessments for students with serious school discipline problems.[43] Research in cognitive psychology provides new clues to the link between thinking and behavior.

Alfred Adler was among the first to note that a person's "private logic" can lead to behavior problems.[44] Troubled behavior may result when students use self-defeating coping strategies. They may hunger to belong yet avoid others for fear of rejection. Brutalized children may see adults as predators and act with hypervigilance. Distrustful individuals may erroneously attribute malice to others.[45]

John Seita suffered repeated abandonment as a child and came to see all adults as the hated enemy. He battled everyone in authority with weapons of *fight, flight,* or *fool*. Here he describes the strategies of attack, retreat, or deception used to outwit adults:

> I chose my behavior to fit the circumstances. Sometimes I sulked and withdrew; other times I was angry and explosive. Most of the time I was sneaky. If it served my purposes, I could even be compliant. It was all a big game. In many ways I felt that I was above consequences. Short of killing me, there was nothing anybody could do to me that was as devastating than what had already happened. Adults tried to punish, bribe, and sweet-talk me into being what they wanted me to be. Loss of privileges, isolation, spankings, and threats only solidified my belief that nobody can be trusted.[46]

John's behavior frustrated adults but served a purpose that made sense to him. Adults had hurt John many times before and now he drove them away. This was a short-term victory, since in his words, "I was in relationship hell."

A new boy came to our school wearing a cap that read, "Shoot me. I'm already dead." This is a cry of spiritual crisis. Many youth search for answers to the most basic existential questions: Why was I born? What value am I to anyone? Sixteen-year-old Tyrone explains:

> A lot of times I think I'm dead. You might as well say I am. The only difference in being dead is I feel I would be a lot better off at times. Not having to

worry about going out and hurting someone. A lot of times I feel I would be dead if it wasn't for my family and God. A lot of times I don't even know why God put me on the earth. I don't feel like I've accomplished anything but hurting people.

Moral development researcher John Gibbs has identified four distortions in thinking that weaken conscience and lead children into antisocial behavior.[47] As shown in the accompanying list of **cognitive distortions**, the core problem is *self-centered thinking*. A person selfishly guards his or her own immediate desires while disregarding perspectives of others: "When somebody has what I want, it's mine." Second, in *minimizing* or *mislabeling*, antisocial behavior becomes harmless or cool, while people are given demeaning labels: "He's just a wuss, we gave him what he deserved." Third, in *assuming the worst*, hostile intentions are attributed to others and many believe it is inevitable that bad things will happen: "People will stab you in your back if you don't watch out." The fourth thinking error is

Cognitive Distortions

1. **Self-centered**—The according of status to one's own views, expectations, needs, rights, immediate feelings, and desires to such an extent that the legitimate views, etc., of others (or even one's own long-term best interests) are scarcely considered or are disregarded altogether.

2. **Minimizing/Mislabeling**—Depicting antisocial behavior as causing no real harm or being acceptable or even admirable, or referring to others with belittling or dehumanizing labels.

3. **Assuming the Worst**—Misattributing hostile intentions to others, considering a worst-case scenario for a social situation as if it were inevitable, or assuming that improvement is impossible in one's own or others' behavior.

4. **Blaming Others**—Misattributing blame for one's harmful actions to outside sources, especially to another person, a group, or a momentary aberration (one was drunk, high, in a bad mood, etc.), or misattributing blame for one's victimization or other misfortune to innocent others.

blaming, refusing to own one's own behavior while shifting responsibility to others: "If he didn't want his money stolen, he shouldn't flash it around."

Most students who seem to lack remorse for hurting others know right from wrong but their thinking errors justify their actions. Albert Bandura describes how students invent elaborate moral justifications for behavior such as, "It's all right to steal to help your family." They also may use a false standard to judge their own morality: "Others do a lot worse things than I do."[48] This dark thinking minimizes evil acts or even recasts these as virtues. Bullies beat up weak people to prove their manhood. Satanic cults embrace sin to please the devil. Adolescents take pride in defiant behavior.

Fighting Back

I hated all the people at the school and I'm loving that I hate these people. It was negative energy that felt good for some reason. I kept making other people feel bad. I felt they deserved it because in some way they tried to hurt me or I thought they tried to hurt me.

—Kevin[49]

Problem behavior supported by distorted thinking is highly resistant to change. Many students do not respond in "reasonable" ways to correction or punishment but only become angry. They interpret legitimate criticism as an attack. Once in a power struggle, all parties find it hard to disengage. Young people don't want to give in to adults. Adults don't want to surrender to defiance. In short order, the battle is engaged.

Punishment works for some, but backfires with others. Hostile encounters can contaminate relationships and even lead to physical aggression. Some youngsters see punishment as a way of proving toughness: "Go ahead, hit me, see if I care." One girl described how she enjoyed provoking adults into angry, emotional encounters: "I wanted to make my teachers feel as miserable as I felt." Strong-willed youth pride themselves on taking what we dish out. They refuse to submit and would probably spit all the way to the electric chair. A few get pleasure from suffering. A young person said, "I like getting beat; it's the same feeling I get when I cut on myself."

All humans learn from natural consequences. But when we believe somebody else is trying to cause us pain, we are likely to feel hate toward the punisher instead of remorse for our actions. Some students deny responsibility, blame the punishing adult and plot revenge. Marty fumed about getting back at the assistant principal who suspended him: "He has a new car; wait until I get through with it." Others use punishment as proof they are bad and worthless. Denise told detention center staff, "I am a total f--- up. I keep disappointing my parents. I deserve being locked up. I should never have been born." Punishment can make children sneakier. A student expelled for smoking said, "I won't be so dumb as to get caught next time." We once received a note from a student that read: "Your staff treat me like shit. By the time you read this, I'll be long gone. And don't think you can find me either!"

Punishment is toxic to children who have suffered rejection and abuse. Fred Tully describes Rocky, a primitive five-year old who had been removed from an abusive, alcoholic mother and subsequently failed in 30 foster placements. It soon became obvious why teachers and foster parents gave up with such regularity. His behavior was dangerous, and he would have to be physically removed to keep him from hurting other children or himself. He then provoked restraint and would dig his nails into the adult's arms, kick, and bite. Because of his age, he couldn't explain his frustration, but he certainly showed his feelings in actions. Rocky has been unable to bond to teachers or surrogate parents. He never knows where he will be next and who will take care of him. Seething with rage, he is devoid of any sense of self-worth.[50]

Historically, punishment has been used against people of lower status and is intertwined with racism. Children of color are at much greater risk of academic failure, discipline sanctions, and dropping out. Mike Williams, who directs community programs for troubled youth, reported that his own daughter came home from her first day in elementary school in tears. She said that the teacher had chastised a new African American boy for being disruptive and made him sit up front with girls rather than in the back with boys. When he resisted this move, she sent him to the principal's office. After only one day, he was on the skids to educational failure.

Discipline of children of color is not always culturally relevant, says Williams. Many of these children have spent their entire lives in fear. From zero to five, they live in dangerous tenements and are locked inside. Parents try to protect their children by hiding them like moles. Nurtured in fear, they become hyper-vigilant and see the world as a combat zone. In school, they play roughly, are loud, and don't obey. Adults fear these children, and since they are too young to kick out, we send them to special education or medicate them. In one suburban elementary school in an inner-city area, 78 percent of African American males were on medications for hyperactivity and learning disorders. Williams is frustrated that policy makers ignore these problems: "Racism is driving our kids crazy. Where is the uproar about a system that says, 'only about one-third of our kids will succeed?' These kids need hope."

To preserve the social order of a family, school, or community, it may be necessary to administer consequences for serious misbehavior. But one should never assume that punishing kids alone will "teach them a lesson." After a lifetime studying the unintended side effects of punishment, B. F. Skinner concluded,

"To return to punitive control is to admit that we have failed to solve a central problem in education."[51] Said another way, punishment is a control strategy but not an educational method.

Conclusion

Children who hurt can become children who hate. Reared in disrespect, they don't learn to respect others. The experience of ridicule and racism in school is highly destructive to many students. Those who fail in school often seek out other antisocial peers. These groups are like think tanks of angry youth. They coach one another in hostile thinking and values. Their defiance draws adults into conflict cycles. Punishment often backfires and further alienates adolescents from adults. Youth who are locked in opposing contests with adults cannot use them as mentors.

Works Cited

[1] Gilligan. 1997. Dr. Gilligan is the director of the Center for the Study of Violence at the Harvard Medical School.

[2] The authors first became aware of the Our Lady of Angels story when contacted at Starr Commonwealth in 1978 by Tom Fitzpatrick of the *Chicago Sun Times*. Fitzpatrick was writing a twentieth anniversary feature on the disaster. His investigative reporting made public previously sealed court information about the case of Tony. Our discussion draws from Fitzpatrick's work and the extensive media file of the Our Lady of Angels school disaster provided by the Chicago Public Library. Further information comes from two prior books on the fire: David Cowan and John Kuenster. 1996. *To Sleep with the Angels: The Story of a Fire*. Chicago: Ivan R. Dee provides the most thorough background of the boy whom court officials believed was responsible for this fire. For a victim's perspective of the tragedy, see M. McBride. 1979. *The Fire That Will Not Die*. Palm Springs, CA: ETC Publications. We have synthesized information available in the public record through the sources cited above. Nothing has previously been published about the educational and treatment program provided to Tony at Starr Commonwealth. This information was provided by program administrators during Tony's stay: Al Lilly was Director of Clinical Services, and Kent Esbaugh was Director of Education. Prior

authors have protected Tony's identity, and we continue to respect that confidentiality by altering identifying data.

[3] Kanner. 1957. Also see, Carin Ness. 2000.

[4] Ramsey. 1943.

[5] Kazdin. 1994.

[6] Nelson and Lewak. 1988.

[7] Simon. 2000.

[8] Marquand. 2001.

[9] Sherman. 1993.

[10] Tyler. 1990.

[11] Sherman. 1993.

[12] Braithwaite. 1989.

[13] Sherman. 1993.

[14] Goldstein. 1999b.

[15] Goldstein. 1999a.

[16] Selye. 1978.

[17] Goldstein. 1999a.

[18] Walsh and Beyer. 1987.

[19] Montague. 1978.

[20] Heilbrun and Heilbrun, 1985.

[21] Petit and Brooks. 1998.

[22] Athens. 1992.

[23] Kipnis. 1999.

[24] Kipnis. 1999.

[25] Sadker and Sadker. 1994.

[26] Personal communication with Linda Lantieri of the Resolving Conflict Creatively Program.

[27] Olweus. 1978.

[28] Hoover and Olson. 2000.

[29] Beck. 1999.

[30] Gibbs, Potter, Goldstein, and Brendtro. 1998.

[31] Pipher. 1996.

[32] Nichols. 1996.

[33] Berkey, Keyes, and Longhurst. 2001.

[34] Sanders. 1970.

[35] Addams. 1909.

[36] Gold and Osgood. 1992.

[37] Portions of this discussion are drawn from John Gibbs, G. Bud Potter, Arnold Goldstein, and Larry Brendtro. 1996. From Harassment to helping with antisocial youth. *Reclaiming Children and Youth* 5(1):40–46.

[38] Morrison. 2000.

[39] Katz. 1993.

[40] Guthrie and McClellan. 2000.

[41] Quirk and Wood. 1999.

[42] Nichols and Shaw. 1999.

[43] Whitt, Daly, and Noell. 2000.

[44] Seita and Brendtro. 2001.

[45] Dodge, Lochman, Harnish, Bates, and Petit. 1997.

[46] Seita and Brendtro. 2001.

[47] Gibbs, Potter, and Goldstein. 1995.

[48] Bandura, Barbaranelli, Caprara, and Pastorelli. 1996.

[49] Kevin was a student in an alternative school who turned his life around. Adapted in his account in Edna Olive. 1999.

[50] Tully and Brendtro. 1998.

[51] Skinner. 1989.

chapter two

Kids in Crisis

I'm afraid to tell you who I am because I'm the only me I've got and you might not like it.

—Patricia, age 13[1]

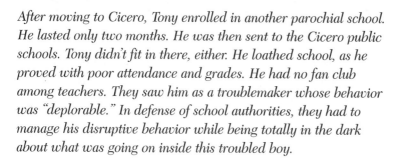

After moving to Cicero, Tony enrolled in another parochial school. He lasted only two months. He was then sent to the Cicero public schools. Tony didn't fit in there, either. He loathed school, as he proved with poor attendance and grades. He had no fan club among teachers. They saw him as a troublemaker whose behavior was "deplorable." In defense of school authorities, they had to manage his disruptive behavior while being totally in the dark about what was going on inside this troubled boy.

Tony's new stepfather tried to lay down the law. But he didn't give Tony the love he craved. When it was just Tony and his mom, home had been a sanctuary from a hostile world. With the new man in the house, home became a battleground. Tony's behavior continued to deteriorate.

Tony was repeatedly seen in the vicinity of suspicious Cicero fires. When questioned, he denied involvement. He was never detained or locked up but always released to his mother. She apparently denied or minimized his behavior and sought to protect him. In her view, he showed guilt or remorse and didn't know what he was doing.

Tony wasn't a kid without a conscience. Close bonds to his mother and his religious training gave him the capacity to feel guilt when he hurt others. But when trouble is a reaction to inner turmoil, piling on guilt only increases disturbance. Threats and punishment also backfire by heightening the stress that triggers acting out.

According to neighbors, Tony's stepfather was abusive. He reportedly beat Tony with rabbit punches and held his hand over the gas burner. Tony was terrified of the man who told him: "The next time you set anything on fire and if you kill anybody, and if the police don't get you and give you the electric chair, I'll come after you myself and kill you."

The Angels fire occurred on the first of December, a date that Tony didn't forget. In the weeks around the third anniversary of the Angels tragedy Tony was implicated in a string of suspicious fires. He seemed to want to be caught. On the other hand, he was terrified of what his stepfather might do. When interrogated by police, Tony was usually accompanied by his mother, and he denied any wrongdoing.

By now, Tony's mother was so concerned, she rarely let her son out of her sight. She drove him to school so he didn't get into trouble on the way. When she was not working, she accompanied Tony on his paper route for fear he might be accused of some new charge. She also brought him for counseling at Catholic Social Services. His deepest problems remained concealed.

One day Tony knocked on the door of a customer on his paper route. He asked her if she smelled smoke on his clothing. He then reported that he had just "discovered" a fire in a nearby basement and told her to call the fire department. Officials questioned him about this and other fires. They were particularly interested in a blaze that destroyed a bowling alley near his home. A 23-year-old man who roomed with Tony's family died in the blaze. Tony's parents told investigators that he was at home watching TV the night of that fire.

Tony's past caught up to him on December 8, 1961. He admitted to police that he set some fires in Cicero. Tony described one fire where the motive seems to have been retribution: "I wanted to get even with the kid who lives there. He pushes me around a lot and I don't like him." He later recanted this statement.

As investigators zeroed in on Tony, his parents hired an attorney. His mother vigorously protested that her boy was being harassed and pestered by authorities. She charged that they were interrogating him at school whenever there was a fire and interfering with his education. She had kept a list of 11 such fires. She conceded he might have started one or two of them, but certainly he had not started them all.

At the suggestion of their attorney, the parents agreed to a polygraph test. They hoped to clear the boy of some allegations. Their attorney retained John E. Reid, a prominent polygraph expert, lawyer, and former Chicago police officer.

Mr. Reid was highly skillful and in short order built rapport with Tony. Reid dazzled him with the wonders of a machine that could tell if a boy was lying. The questions about the bowling alley fire were inconclusive. However, Tony readily admitted to setting several lesser fires in his neighborhood. He also recalled details from when he burned a garage when he was only five years old. Tony seemed relieved to be able to get his terrible secrets off his chest. "Sometimes, after I set the fires, I feel so bad I wish I hadn't been born."

When Tony mentioned that he once was a student at Our Lady of Angels school, Mr. Reid was stunned. If this was arson, it was the most infamous incident of school violence in history. Tony was opening up by layers. He initially said only that he knew who set the Angels fire and that he and a friend had talked about it. "On the afternoon it happened, I was coming back to school with this other kid, and I said, 'I got some matches in my pocket and I could burn down the school and we wouldn't have to go to school no more.'"

Mr. Reid played to Tony's conscience: "You know telling a lie is a sin. There are 92 children and three nuns looking down at us right now from heaven who want the truth. Now tell me, did you set the school on fire?"

Tony repeated his conversation about a friend setting the fire. Mr. Reid suspected the boy had created an alter ego and was describing himself. "Son," he said, "I don't think there's any other kid at all in this case."

Suddenly the "friend" became Tony himself. He told of leaving class to go to the boys' bathroom in the basement and lighting a barrel of paper with three matches. He watched the flames get bigger and bigger and then ran back to his room.

"Why did you set the fire?" Mr. Reid asked. The boy's voice turned bitter: "Because of my teachers," he said. "I hated my teachers and my principal. They always were threatening me. They always wanted to expel me from school."

After speaking to Tony's mother, Mr. Reid determined that she had suspected this all along. Although employed by the family, Reid felt obligated to contact authorities. Joseph Reid related the boy's admission to juvenile judge Alfred Cilella.

On January 16, 1962, the Chicago Tribune reported: "Information that a 13-year-old boy has confessed setting the fire at Our Lady of Angels school which took the lives of 92 children and three nuns was given yesterday to Judge Alfred J. Cilella of Family Court." This was the last the public would hear of the matter for a generation.

The judge sealed all records and ordered that Tony be locked in Audy juvenile home in Chicago. He was held in complete isolation from other youth. Even police and investigators were not

*allowed to interview him. A mental status examination was
ordered. The court psychologist found that Tony scored in the
bright-normal range on the Wechsler Intelligence Scale. A panel
of psychiatrists determined Tony was not psychotic and was
competent to stand trial.*

*It would have been easier for the judge if the youth had been
found mentally ill. What should happen to a highly troubled,
habitual fire-setter? How could the community be protected?
What was in the best interests of this boy?*

*Closed juvenile court hearings began in early February. On
advice of his attorneys, Tony pled not guilty to all charges. He
claimed he gave a confession to Reid because he was frightened
and tired. Under Illinois law of the time, a ten-year-old could
not be held criminally liable. The boy obviously needed mental
health treatment. It was uncertain whether he had intended to
harm anyone.*

*At the completion of the trial phase, Judge Cilella found Tony
guilty of certain Cicero fires. He threw out the Angels charge,
citing inconsistencies in the boy's story. In reality, nothing would
have been served by reopening this tragedy.*

*The judge had few options. He might have committed the boy to
the children's ward of the Chicago State Hospital, a century-old
snake pit that was infamous for abuses.[2] If he placed Tony in the
juvenile corrections system, he was likely to be abused by other
delinquents. The Illinois State Training School at St. Charles was
the spawning ground for delinquent youth gangs that still exist
today.[3] In fact, placement anywhere in Illinois increased the risk
that someone might tie the boy to the Angels fire. He would likely be murdered if his identity were widely known. This suggested that placement outside of the state of Illinois might be in the
best interests of the child. In the very city where the world's first
juvenile court was founded, Judge Alfred J. Cilella faced the
most important decision of his career.*

The Pessimism Lens

This country seems to have only two policy formulations for teens. One is control . . . and the other is repair. Neither talks about a policy that claims youth and asks youth to contribute positively as equal partners.

—John Calhoun, National Crime Prevention Council[4]

For a century there has been strong disagreement about the best strategy for dealing with youth in conflict. Two polarized positions have emerged, *punishment* and *rehabilitation*. Briefly, the battle lines are drawn like this:

Punishment approaches deal with youth in conflict as disruptive and dangerous. In this view, youth only respond to force so the solution is to *get tough*. This has led to zero-tolerance schools and wars on delinquency.

Rehabilitation typically treats youth in conflict as disturbed and deficient. These youngsters aren't normal but are victims damaged by nature or nurture. With such a view, the solution is *flaw-fixing* by diagnosing and treating deficits.

Both punishment and rehabilitation seek to stomp out problems. Both are reactive and preoccupied with deviance and deficit. On closer inspection, these apparent opposites turn out to be remarkably similar in outlook. We refer to this mindset as the *Pessimism Lens*. The focus is on what is wrong with youth rather than what their strengths and potentials might be.

Threat and Hostility

Conflict can be viewed either as an opportunity or as a threat.
Seen through the pessimism lens, conflict produces fight or
flight behavior. Nearly a century ago, sociologist Emile
Durkheim observed that, whatever the intellectual rationaliza-
tion, punishment is first and foremost an instinctual, emotional
reaction to threat. This reflexive response once had survival
value but is now mostly a crude weapon that blocks reflective
action.[5] When threat triggers hostile instincts, it is virtually
impossible to activate the contrary instincts of empathy.
Depending on which instinct rules, the individual adopts a mindset of either *understanding* or *hostility*. Those prejudiced by hostility find it impossible to "hate the sin and love the sinner."[6]

As humans, we wish to solve a difficult problem rationally, we
do it by using the frontal lobes of our brain. But in moments of
threat, we shift down to the "reptilian" brain, a primitive survival center that programs us for fight or flight. Most of the pro-
posals for dealing with adolescents who frustrate adults are fight
or flight responses.

For millennia, the remedy for violence was violence. Under
Roman law, the patriarch had absolute authority to harshly
punish or even get rid of an obstinate offspring. Virtually any
means of inflicting pain was justified if used by those in
authority against those of inferior status, including wives,
serfs, sailors, slaves, and, of course, children. While most of
these groups have won legal rights, racism, sexism, and child
abuse are still common.

Among democracies, the United States is lawless unto itself in
its approach to defiant and delinquent children. The U.S.
Supreme Court still maintains that it is legal for schools to
physically punish or expel students. Large numbers of juveniles
are locked in adult jails and prisons. Children can be sentenced
to life imprisonment or execution. In 1910, Winston Churchill
observed that the mood and temper of a nation's treatment of
people who violate its laws is an unfailing test of civilization.[7]
By this standard, the world's most powerful nation flunks.

Advocates of harsh punishment employ thinking errors similar to criminals; they disregard the well-being of those they wish to hurt. James Gilligan of the Harvard Center for the Study of Violence contends that the motives and goals that underlie crime are the same that underlie punishment. The criminal and the court both seek justice to avenge perceived injuries and injustices.[8]

A student who senses hostility is primed to respond in kind. Pioneering school psychologist John Morgan noted that children dislike those adults who make them feel unintelligent, fearful, or ashamed. This dislike becomes hostility if the students think they have been unfairly treated. When the adult's motive for punishment is retribution, the child correctly concludes that this is a hostile act. The child feels justified in resentment and hatred.[9]

Demonizing Youth

Retribution rhetoric becomes a false expression of masculinity and courage. Rooted in sexist name-calling, those not "tough" on delinquents are mocked as "wimps." Those seeking to understand and reclaim youth in conflict are painted as "emotional" and "soft." Child advocates are "whiners," "do-gooders," and "bleeding hearts" who lack guts. The phrase "social worker" itself becomes a negative term in this decidedly antisocial rhetoric.

The chief New York juvenile prosecutor, Peter Reinharz, labels juvenile offenders as "creeps," "dirt bags," "city shitheads," "depraved," "pintsize predators," and "scum of the earth." Teens who appear to show remorse are actually "clever liars," and don't deserve special attention:

> The schools may move him to an alternative program filled with other predators, but they will still try to educate him. More likely, the education mavens will classify him as emotionally disturbed and place him in a special education program. There he can enjoy high teacher to student ratios and special programs and curricula developed on

behalf of muggers, robbers, rapists, drug dealers, and other nefarious types.[10]

This official of the New York juvenile court mocks advocates of troubled youth as "do goodniks" and treats their parents as trash. He demonizes disturbed young people as mental misfits who mock the court, smirking and laughing in tones so chilling, it is as if the devil himself were laughing. Presumably, Reinharz uses such rhetoric while prosecuting juveniles. If jurors swallow his rubbish, they will treat juveniles as disposable garbage.

Youth bashing rose to the level of national policy when Alfred Regnery was appointed to head the Office of Juvenile Justice and Delinquency Prevention. In the journal *Crime and Delinquency*, he announced that it was no longer the government's role to solve delinquency as a social problem. Instead, the new federal role was "making the predators accountable."[11] Such youth bashing panders to the thinking errors of blaming and assuming the worst.

In *The Scapegoat Generation*, social ecologist Michael Males debunks the public's misperception that most crime is caused by juveniles. Whatever problems youth have, adults are likely to have them in greater degree and to have caused them in young people. Teens account for just one percent of illegal drug deaths. Adult males have impregnated most of those who become unwed school-age mothers. When a child is murdered, the perpetrator is most likely to be an adult. Young people serve 60 percent longer sentences than adults do for the same crime.[12]

Many adults believe that "a whack worked for me and that's what today's kids need." In their view, schools have problems with disrespectful students because "we aren't allowed to lay a hand on them." However, educational literature for two centuries is replete with evidence that the most respected teachers were those who treated students respectfully. Young people fear but don't respect persons who knock them around.

The logical flaw in harsh punishment for violence is that it teaches violence. Certainly, without sanctions for antisocial behavior, any society would degenerate into chaos. It is the strength of human bonds, however, not the severity of punishment, which preserves social order. In fact, extreme punishment is one of the most blatant symptoms of decaying social order.

Chest-Beating Propaganda

Demeaning with labels is a classic propaganda technique. The first step in dehumanization is name-calling. Psychologist Gordon Allport noted that prejudice proceeds in five degrading stages. These are listed below with examples from the youth bashing language: [13]

1. Speak against: *He is a worthless punk.*

2. Avoid: *Keep her away from the good kids.*

3. Discriminate: *They don't belong in this school.*

4. Attack: *All they understand is force.*

5. Exterminate: *We're finished with you.*

Prejudicial labels cloud rational discourse. The national press widely reported a Michigan proposal for a "punk prison" to incarcerate juveniles. The term "punk" is insulting in common use, but in prison it is a violent term, denoting an inmate targeted for rape. The use of "punks" and "predators"—words to denigrate and discard troubled youth—is itself an act of violence. By exploiting fear of violence, one can stifle voices of reason.

The media can stir public hostility by the way they cast their stories. During a conference on youth problems in New Zealand, a Wellington newspaper headline blared, "Boy Rapist Sent to Adult Court."[14] The article described how a woman was abducted at knifepoint and raped by a man and a 14-year-old boy. Deep in the article, the reader learned that the boy had suffered sexual abuse in foster placements and, in fact, the adult charged in the rape was a former foster father of this boy. How different the target of public outrage would be if the newspaper headline had read, "State-Approved Foster Parent Leads Young Boy Into Kidnapping and Rape."

Religion is the guardian of faith and values but can mutate into hateful propaganda. Messages of compassion and brotherly love are drowned out by moralistic vindictiveness.[15] Scott Larson and Larry Brendtro describe the spiritual emptiness of many of our modern day "prodigal sons and daughters." Faith communities can be key players in spiritual development.[16] How tragic, then, when religion turns troubled youth into outcasts. There can be no more fundamental moral value than reclaiming our prodigal sons and daughters.

Throughout history, propagandists have used fear to justify violence toward fellow humans. When angry emotions are ignited, the result is a hatred-driven vindictiveness, as seen in the Crusades, the concentration camps, and the bitterness of racial hatred. The Golden Rule is revoked by the psychology of vengeance. Punishments are an essential part of the social fabric of any society, but they must be administered in a manner that restores the wayward to the community. The notion that one can punish the devil out of a person is flawed psychology and religion. As Martin Luther reflected, a person who is converted by fear remains unconverted.

Conflict in the Schools

The narrowness of the school enclosure induces many a boy to jump the fence.

—Jane Addams, 1909[17]

At-risk and troubled students bring all the social ills of our society into the classrooms, causing teachers to feel overwhelmed and helpless. The volume and intensity of inappropriate behaviors poses alarming problems for teachers. The majority of troubled students are not being served by effective inclusion, nor are they participating in quality alternative or therapeutic school programs. Most are languishing, fighting, and disrupting the education programs in their schools. We have observed more primitive and bizarre student behavior in the public schools than we have ever witnessed in our residential facilities.

Mainstreaming or Mainscreaming

For decades, schools have been challenged to incorporate emotionally handicapped students in regular classes under concepts of "integration," "normalization," "mainstreaming," or "total inclusion." There have been some gains but mostly resistance to this philosophy. Inclusion did not begin with regular classroom teachers but was an externally imposed reform movement.[18]

Many mandates for school reforms work at cross-purposes. Teachers are pushed to raise test scores; they are also assigned very troubled students but are not given support or specialized training. This is a recipe for stress and failure. When a teacher was to be sent an emotionally disturbed student from a treatment center, she responded, "If I have to take Jason into my classroom, this placement will be called mainscreaming and not mainstreaming."[19]

Public schools are trying to manage even the most disturbed students, sometimes with primitive methods. The upscale community of Marshall, Michigan, put disruptive students in "the box." In the corner of a special education classroom was a box about the size of a windowless phone booth. It was designed for use with disruptive, emotionally impaired children who bite, punch, or swear.

Nobody is sure who started the idea of the box, but other schools use something similar. Says a school psychologist, "Most educators would rather use the time-out booth than to have to physically restrain the child." A principal in another school explains that her time-out cell is really "a room like a small classroom, about seven foot by five foot, heated and with lighting, but no desk or chairs. We feel it's a good tool in dealing with aggressive students who are using foul language or being abusive." Dr. Charles Smith from the University of Kansas supports separation of children who are losing control but sees the

Artwork and poem by Ann

My mind spins round and round
Marked by scarlet
Filled with hatred,
Hatred of life.
And here I detest the mirror's demented pictures.
I am lanced with confusion
And mocked by happiness,
Leaving only anger,
Using it as a cover,
As the thorns protecting the soft petals of a black rose.

box as designed to intimidate and create terror. "Putting a child into a box is not a good practice regardless of the child's problem. It is not only archaic, it is cruel."[20]

The theory of inclusion was to give teachers support so that challenging students could succeed with their normal peers. An example of a pure integration model comes from an Italian school where a behaviorally handicapped child is sent into a regular classroom team-taught by special educators. The American brand of inclusion is often just a plot to curtail services and costs. Under the guise of "least restrictive alternative," some children are in fact highly restricted.

Discarding Students at Risk

In its original meaning, the term "at risk" was meant to focus attention on the hazards in the environment, not characteristics of youth. But as Michele Fine noted, the language of risk was twisted to communicate that these young people are not like us.[21] Conservatives used risk as a rationale for isolating these youth, while liberals saw risk as a means of displaying them. Both operated from fear.

The at-risk movement fueled the development of alternative schools with great variation in quality. We recently visited one large urban district where 4,000 students come to an alternative center one hour per week to have their schoolwork checked. If they fulfill this task, they may be allowed back into a full-time alternative school. The strongest criticism of alternative schools is not that they fail students, but that they stream into dysfunctional high schools.[22] Purged of troublemakers, depersonalized and factory schools herd along the adolescents who want to meet adult expectations.

Ever since the passage of compulsory school attendance laws, schools have found loopholes to permit discarding disruptive students. Rather than change the nature of education, schools remove those who disrupt classroom order. Most of these students have behavior and learning disabilities. Some schools hire consultants who show school boards clever tricks for not identifying such children. Such students often end up imprisoned in the juvenile justice system.[23]

Schools are required to develop *zero-reject* policies for special needs students. Many are more concerned with *zero-tolerance*.

Let's make it clear, we don't agree with those who say schools should be tolerant of destructive behavior. Most parents don't tolerate drug use, disrespect, or violence in their families with their own children. But neither do they throw them out of the house if problems arise. The catchy term "zero-tolerance" has become a code word for disciplining by discarding. If we treat children badly anywhere, soon we will treat children badly everywhere. If we use punishing approaches, we pass them on across generations.

There must be high standards for behavior, but it is a double standard to hold children accountable while letting adults off the hook. Depriving children of an education is educational malpractice. John Goodlad says that education will finally be a moral profession when it stops expelling students to nowhere.[24] If medical professionals were to strap difficult cases to a gurney and push them into the street without treatment, it would be called patient abandonment. To expel teenagers to the streets is an act of violence condemning these young people to be failures in their lives and threats to the rest of us.

Instead of providing special services, some schools are criminalizing misbehavior by transforming unfortunate schoolyard conflicts into violations of the criminal code—doing whatever it takes to get rid of a particularly disruptive child. What once might have been seen as a playground fistfight becomes battery, and threats and profanity become assault. These are serious problems, but we wonder how any responsible educator might think the criminal justice system can raise children better than schools.

In the panic after highly publicized school violence, there has been a burgeoning industry in antiviolence programs. Arnold Goldstein counts as many as 300 approaches, most products of hearsay, hope, and desperation rather than sound evaluation.[25] The most popular response to aggression is punishment. This is not just the benign type like a short time out, but rather suspension, expulsion, and even corporal punishment. In a recent year, at least 15 percent of eighth-grade boys nationwide were suspended or expelled from school, and as many as half the male black students in many urban schools suffered that fate.[26] Physical punishment of children in schools is permitted in 23 states, where three-quarters of a million such incidents occur annually. Imagine the outrage if there were 750,000 physical assaults by students on teachers or principals! In addition to the popular paddle, punishment is applied with hands, fists, straps, hoses, bats, forced exercise drills, and forcing students to eat noxious substances.[27]

Reprimands are the most frequent interventions used by elementary and junior high teachers, delivering one reprimand every two minutes. Sometimes these yield short-term results, but the chronically disruptive student becomes more defiant under a barrage of parental and teacher criticism.

Educators are sometimes quick to give up on challenging students. Like airlines that report on-time arrivals, schools should be graded based on their "holding power" with challenging students. A study at Harvard University found there are severe dropout problems in the largest U.S. cities. At the time of this study, ten major cities reported a majority of their schools had a holding power of less than 50 percent. That means that a majority of students who entered as freshmen did not graduate with their class. These problems are most serious in schools with more than 900 students, where the majority is predominantly black or Latino. John Grossman is the president of the Columbus Ohio Education Association, a district where 65 percent of schools had a holding power of less than 50 percent. He suggests that administrators are under pressure to force poor achievers out of school rather than have them drag down test results that help determine cash bonuses. There is an incentive to get rid of these students, said Grossman.[28]

After a lifetime of training teachers to work with disruptive students, Frank Wood concludes that traditional educational interventions have been conspicuously ineffective. Aggressive and noncompliant students frustrate us by *doing* what we forbid. Passive-aggressive youth frustrate us by *not doing* what we want. Why do they fight us so? Many think their current coping behaviors serve them better than the alternatives we are urging.

Others believe their situation is so hopeless that their only choices are to fight or give up.[29]

It is not just disadvantaged students who find school irrelevant. Reed Larson of the University of Illinois obtained self-reports from middle class adolescents. He equipped them with pagers, and when signaled, students recorded their activities and attitudes. Students reported being bored over a quarter of the time. Both delinquents and honor students had much higher rates of boredom, often over half of the random moments. Reed concludes that this is not psychopathology but a lack of opportunity for positive youth development. Without engagement in positive activities, young people get turned on by drugs, promiscuous sexuality, and delinquency. The central task facing educators is to find how to get the fires of adolescence lit.[30]

Crisis in the Courts

Thus we see society almost helpless in the grip of the hostile attitude it has taken toward those who break its laws and contravene its institutions. Hostility toward the lawbreaker inevitably brings with it the attitudes of retribution, repression, and exclusion.

—George Herbert Mead, 1918[31]

At the beginning of the twentieth century, courts in all democratic countries were redesigned to balance the best interests of the child with public safety. By the end of the century, this process was being reversed in the United States by clamors to protect the public and punish the children. Behind this move were many critics of rehabilitation, both conservatives and liberals. Conservatives contend that this is an outmoded nineteenth century liberal philosophy that is overly optimistic about human nature. Who can really believe there is no such thing as a bad boy amidst the reality of youth violence? The classic view of the child as victim rescues troublemakers, excuses their behavior, and fails to hold them accountable. In their view, a far better "treatment" is punishment.

On another front, liberals attack juvenile courts for being paternalistic and authoritarian. The doctrine of "parens patriae" allows government to take over the responsibility of parenting delinquents and status offenders such as runaways. This has created massive injustices where children are denied the protection afforded adults. For example, we worked with an individual who was incarcerated for a minor theft in school and was locked up for most of five years because he kept fighting his "rehabilitation."

Many rehabilitation efforts are little more than disguised retribution. Perhaps the most valid criticism of the juvenile court is that it has strayed far from the spirit of its founders. Under the leadership of Jane Addams in Chicago of 1899, the modern juvenile court was created. Almost nobody in the juvenile justice debate seems to be clear about its original purpose. The mission statement of the children's court is reproduced here as a reality check:

The Juvenile Court Purpose: Cook County, Illinois, 1899

> To secure for each minor subject hereto such care and guidance, preferably in his own home, as will serve the moral, emotional, mental, and physical welfare of the minor and the best interests of the community.
>
> To preserve and strengthen the minor's family ties whenever possible, removing him from the custody of his parents only when his welfare or safety or protection of the public cannot be adequately safeguarded without removal.

When the minor is removed from his own family, to secure for him custody, care, and discipline as nearly as possibly equivalent to that which should be given by his parents.

Remarkably, the document doesn't even mention rehabilitation or treatment. Instead, the goal is meeting the needs of young people, balanced with public safety.

The juvenile court was founded on principles of positive youth development. But for a half century, the focus in delinquency research has been on negative development, in other words, relapsing into criminal behavior. Hundreds of studies have shown that treatment often fails to turn delinquents around. This led some to contend that "nothing works" in rehabilitation. Robert Martinson, who popularized this view in the 1970s, later retracted these conclusions. They still are cited by advocates of punishment. Many treatment interventions can be effective. No credible studies suggest that punishment is effective, a fact conveniently ignored by "nothing works" fans.

The debate on punishment versus compassion is gender-tainted. Those who want to help difficult juveniles are "soft" on crime while those who cry out for punishment are "tough." According to Carol Gilligan, there are two voices of morality.[32] The predominant male voice calls for *justice* and is rooted in a focus on power. The female voice calls for *caring* and conveys the central importance of human relationships. Both justice and compassion are the foundations of all great ethical systems. But there are dramatic gender preferences. Very few men focus on care in moral decision making while at least half of women do. When males dominate institutions and laws, the caring voice is muted. If half the lawmakers were mothers, would public policy tolerate discarding children?

Juvenile courts are at a turning point. In contradictory reforms, some jurisdictions are still building youth prisons. Others are reversing the trend by creating a range of programs to serve children in their own homes and schools. Those needing secure care are placed in small community-based centers where they can keep in close contact with families. Studies by the National

Council on Crime and Delinquency show that young people have not abused such opportunities. Locking up adolescents has nothing to do with levels of crime; it is a political choice.[33]

Betraying the Young

Having denied children the kind of care and protection that all young human animals must have, we then decide to punish them, in essence for our failure to raise them in the first place . . .. Has there ever been a plan so exquisitely calculated to visit the sins of the fathers upon the children and their children's children?

—Mary Sykes Wylie[34]

According to Amnesty International, the United States, which led the world in creating children's courts, now seems uncertain if kids in trouble should be reclaimed or discarded.[35] Their study, *Betraying the Young*, documents violations of international law governing the rights of troubled juveniles in all states.

"Get tough" quickly degenerates into "get mean" when juveniles are sent to boot camps or lockups, which lack trained staff and educational or youth development resources. Many juveniles are being transferred into the adult system. Another mean-spirited innovation is to import security procedures from adult corrections into juvenile facilities. Razor wire, solitary confinement, shackles, and stun guns have reshaped some juvenile programs into corrupt clones of abusive adult prisons. Thousands of children are being segregated in programs that violate their most basic needs. One such youth said, "A warehouse is a place to keep property so it won't be damaged. In here, the guards and inmates treat me like crap. This isn't a warehouse, it is a garbage dump."

By the mid-twentieth century, only totalitarian countries still locked up huge portions of their populations. Yet in the wake of student unrest during the Viet Nam era, politicians discovered the image-polishing benefits of declaring war on long-haired drug users. New York Governor Nelson Rockefeller was advised that, to be a credible presidential candidate, he had to get tough on crime. Abandoning delinquency prevention, Rockefeller called for locking up small-time drug users. Other politicians followed his lead, and thus began the largest incarceration of citizens by any democracy in the history of the world.

The crime war proved popular as political "leaders" marched in lock-step to the chest-beating cadence. Mandatory sentences and three-strike laws sparked a boom in prison construction. Gang task forces called for trying youngsters as adults and locking them in former military bases in spite of research showing that such sanctions made teens worse.[36] Schools declared "zero-tolerance" for violence by kicking students out into the streets, thereby increasing the probability they would become law-breakers. Black, Latino, and Native American students suffered the brunt of these practices.

During the same time that the U.S. tilted toward punishment, the Correctional Service of Canada changed its goal to success-ful reintegration to the community. America's rate of imprison-ment became the highest on the globe. Bluntly, we have become a nation of jailers. At low levels, imprisonment lowers crime statistics. But once the rate of incarceration in a neigh-borhood exceeds a "tipping" point, perhaps one percent, fami-lies and communities come unraveled and crime rates actually spiral. While America locks away huge numbers of young blacks and Latinos, the neighborhoods they leave behind grow unsta-ble. For example, two percent of America's children must visit prison to see Mom or Dad.[37] We know of many minority schools where at least ten percent of students have a parent in prison. When parents are sent to prison, their children are much more likely to follow.

President Eisenhower once warned of the dangerous power of the military industrial complex. A new corporate correction complex reared its head as youth prison companies were listed on the stock exchanges. These corporations traded political contributions for lucrative contracts allowing them to suck up millions of tax dollars by warehousing youth. They now are the big players, operating a continuum of confinement from shock incarceration for fledgling delinquents to super-max prisons for the "hard core super-predators."

According to Jordan Riak, the real predators are profiteers who operate boot camps that are "torturing teenagers for fun and profit." He provides a listing of young folks who have recently died in what he calls "killer camps." Many are in remote locations and billed as wilderness camps or schools. Others are offshore facilities set up in inaccessible sites without child abuse standards. Youth have nowhere to escape and are isolated from all outside contact, even with their own families.[38] Alexia Parks has documented a litany of such abuses in *An American Gulag: Secret P.O.W. Camps for Teens*. Frustrated parents pay large sums of money to have their children forcibly "escorted" and confined in remote locations.[39]

Walkenhut Incorporated runs Michigan's maximum-security children's prison, complete with two gun towers and a 16-foot perimeter fence reinforced with razor wire. "If we needed to, we could turn this into a supermax facility for the worst adult offenders in two weeks," said the warden.[40] This program houses juveniles who have been tried as adults, some violent and some not. The government is hiring a company to raise these young people, but the focus is solely on security. Said the top turnkey, "The rules weren't written with adolescents in mind. They were written for adults. That's what the public wants for young offenders. I can guarantee we will follow the rules here and provide a safe environment for our staff and the inmates.

That's how I define success. Anything past that, I can't guarantee." Desiree Cooper of the *Detroit Free Press* writes, "Michigan's punitive juvenile policy has marked the end of childhood for hundreds of boys who really never had one."[41]

The trend toward super maximum security and sensory deprivation is called "Marionization" after a maximum-security prison where Mafia chieftains are locked down 23 hours a day. Because of the powerful human need for social attachment to others, solitary confinement is universally used to brainwash prisoners of war. Such practices have led Amnesty International to accuse the United States juvenile justice system of blatant violation of human rights.

Law professor Barry Feld of the University of Minnesota observes that public hostility toward other people's children, especially minority and poor children, has fueled the trend toward punishing children as adults.[42] The sound-bite *do adult crime, serve adult time*, demonstrates massive ignorance of the reality that youth do not think like adults. Feld summarizes numerous research-validated reasons why youth do not yet have the competence and judgment of adults:

1. Youth almost always know right from wrong but have less self-control and ability to manage emotions than adults.

2. Youth do not consider possible long-term risks in the manner that adults do.

3. Having lived less life, youth are more focused on short-term than long-term goals.

4. The temperaments of youth are disposed toward sensation-seeking and excitement.

5. Youth are vulnerable to greater mood variations than adults.

6. Youth are more readily influenced by peers and most misbehavior is group action.

7. Those youth most likely to get in trouble are likely to have their growth delayed by cultural, intellectual, and social disadvantage.

All of these differences are intuitively recognized by adults. No state permits children to be licensed to carry firearms because of universal recognition of their lack of mature judgment.

Further, if punished by incarceration, adolescents experience time differently. A ten-year sentence is but a decade in the life of an adult. To a teen it is equivalent to virtually all the life experiences he or she can remember. Thus, if punishment is to be applied, Feld urges that a "youth discount" be given.

When courts take responsibility for rearing children away from families, then the government becomes the new parent.[43] It is impossible to raise children properly in punishing environments. Adults responsible for young people are obligated to meet their developmental needs.[44] Whether young people suffer abuse from their families or in custody of the state, this is an act of violence.

Psychologist Aaron Kipnis tells of running away as a youth after being abused. He was arrested and placed in a St. Louis detention center. "The guards gave me a thin mattress on the floor in a cell with four young men who filled the double bunks on either side. They began taunting me. The oldest one said that as soon as the lights were out they were going to take turns 'f---ing me in the ass' while I 'sucked their cocks.' Each one of them was larger than me."[45] Later, in Chicago, he witnessed other boys being raped at night or in the showers. Kipnis concludes that our culture has modernized many other archaic institutions to meet the needs of a changing world. The time is long overdue for abandoning an outmoded system. Kipnis notes that the crumbling cell he first occupied in a Los Angeles juvenile hall was built in 1903.

Cruel and Unusual Punishment

To make America safe, you have to identify the criminal, then confine him or kill him.

—Charley Reese[46]

In the wake of a school shooting by a 15-year-old boy, nationally syndicated columnist Reese called for execution or life without parole for serious and repeat offenders. He proposes that both children and adults should be locked down in their cells around the clock. Cells for lifers should be equipped with an I-bolt in the ceiling, six feet of rope, and a short stool. "That way, any time they decide they prefer death to slow rot, they can kill themselves and save us the cost of corn bread and beans."

To execute children or imprison them for life is itself a crime under international law. In 1990, the U.N. Convention on the Rights of the Child prohibited such punishment for offenses committed by children under 18. That same year, Starr Commonwealth hosted an international conference in New York where two dozen nations embraced this document as the conscience of the world. Today, all nations except the U.S. and Somalia—which has no government—have adopted this document. The American Bar Association is also adamant against the penalty of capital punishment for crimes committed by children.[47] Finally, there is solid evidence that even violent juvenile offenders can be reclaimed.[48]

The first recorded child execution on these shores was in Plymouth Colony in 1642. A country boy named Thomas Grauniger was put to death for sexual contact with a cow and a mare. The animals received the same punishment.[49] Since Grauniger, 360 other young people have suffered the same fate.

Twenty-three states permit such punishment. In recent years, almost all executions for child crime have been in the south, with Texas accounting for over half. In a 15-year period, three countries accounted for virtually all known executions for child crimes. The U.S. led with 17; Iraq executed 13 and Iran, five.[50]

There are great inequities in who receives such punishment.[51] Most are minorities and poor. All are males. They typically have records of severe abuse and psychological disturbance as children. Defense lawyers seldom have the training or resources to establish the mitigating circumstances as required under federal law. Only a third of the cases had pretrial psychiatric evaluations, and these were inadequate. The most extensive study of youth awaiting execution documented a chilling malpractice where attorneys in alliance with families agreed to conceal parental physical or sexual abuse to spare further embarrassment.[52]

Solid statistics on the number of children imprisoned for life are not available. Virtually all states permit life sentences without parole for crimes by children. Washington allows eight-year-olds to be sentenced to life, while in Vermont ten-year-olds can qualify. Courts differ on whether this penalty is defined as cruel and unusual punishment. A Nevada court overturned the life sentence of a 13-year-old. Washington upheld such a penalty for another 13-year-old. We worked with 14-year-old Paul Jensen, Jr., who was sentenced by a South Dakota court to life without parole. Amnesty International's report, *Betraying the Young*, begins with a letter that Paul sent to his sentencing judge from prison:

> Judge Zintner: I have an important question to ask you! Would you please move me out of here? Please don't leave me here with all these adults. I can't relate to any of them. They pick on me because I am just a kid. They tease me and taunt me. They talk to me sexually. They make moves on me. I've had people tell me I'm pretty and that they'll rape me. . . . I'm even too scared to go eat. . . . It's too much for anyone my age to handle. . . . Please help me with this.[53]

In the conscience of the world, sentences such as Paul's are cruel and unusual punishment. Meanwhile, he and hundreds like him try to cling to hope when they have no future. The day Paul entered prison he asked, "Do you think in 20 or 30 years the U.S. will change its laws so kids like me can have a life?"

One of the authors of this book is a member of the Coordinating Council on Juvenile Justice and Delinquency Prevention, chaired by the attorney general. The council includes judges, police, and delinquency experts appointed by the president and the two houses of Congress. [54] The council members come from diverse political backgrounds but are unanimous in calling for alternatives to absolute punishment of children. One council member, a southern judge, put it thus: "Most people in my state don't care what the U.N. says, but we are Americans and Americans don't kill their kids!"

Flaw-Fixing Treatment

Psychology and kindred disciplines persistently study the negative (disease, crime, psychopathology, aggression, etc.) and how it might be corrected. Rarely is the focus on strength and its facilitation.

—Arnold Goldstein [55]

For decades psychologists accumulated a massive literature on such topics as anxiety, depression, and aggression, but they know relatively little about the psychology of well-being. This blindness to strengths has led to "anemic programming" for students. [56] Like schools and courts, the mental health field has been preoccupied with deviance and deficit while blind to the strengths and resilience of youth.

Public mental health services have traditionally followed an illness model in which health is characterized as the absence of psychopathology. These services have little validity when it comes to treating our most troubled children and youth. Clinicians are overworked, underpaid, and functioning in a reactive mode. Professional judgment is overruled by mavens of managed care who ration services and rely on drugs to tame rebellious youth. Interventions consist mainly of brief assessments and short-term symptom management. The ideal of a continuum of comprehensive services is a hollow promise. Affordable residential care is a rarity and the prevailing model is to "stabilize and discharge."

The most virulent strain of professional pessimism is low expectations. Assuming the worst, treatment professionals quarantine youth into roles of victim or patient. Those who highlight the *victim status* of an individual provide excuses for irresponsible behavior. Children need empathy and understanding, not adults who feel sorry for them and set low expectations. The *patient role* highlights pathology. Speaking for adolescents like himself who have been in treatment programs, Brian Raychaba of Toronto says: "Young persons must be allowed to be active subjects, not merely objects in somebody else's grand scheme, 'saving young unfortunates.'"[57]

The pessimism of treatment is personified in labels given troubled youth. In the English language, to think in negative ways one only needs to add the prefix *de-* or *dis-*. Psychologists like the word *disordered*, special educators prefer *disabled*, and a favorite of social workers is *dysfunctional*. Psychiatrists have their own list of unfriendly sounding labels published in the ever-expanding DSM series. Scholarly journals are filled with articles on disordered behavior, disturbed emotions, deviant thinking, dysfunctional families, and deprived environments.

Brilliant professional pessimists write books to spread their thinking errors. Criminologists J. Wilson and R. Herrnstein contend that students who are "temperamentally as well as intellectually different" are to blame for eroding educational standards. "When the proportion of low IQ students becomes too high, they then set the tone for the school."[58] They are cynical about rehabilitating antisocial youth and argue for a return to retribution as just and equitable.[59] Presumably, these Harvard professors have been deprived of the opportunity to discover how clever and resourceful kids who outwit adults really can be.

Jonathan Kellerman is a child clinical psychologist turned crime novelist. A testimony to his pessimistic views on adolescents in trouble is his nonfiction book, *Savage Spawn: Reflections on Violent Children*. He produced this for a panicked public after the Columbine school shootings. Kellerman cautions against empathy for antisocial adolescents whom he describes as "a species apart." He likes the label psychopath. "It's a juicy term, connotative of evil, and this is a juicy, evil creature we are dealing with."[60] Once having maligned them, he is ready to discard them: "The chances of eliminating entrenched psychopathic behavior in an adolescent are extremely low if not zero."[61]

The popularization of this junk psychology is infiltrating our schools where more youngsters are viewed as punks and psychopaths rather than young people who possess the potential for greatness. This is prejudice masquerading as behavioral science. Experts who have studied conscience development find that even among delinquents, nine out of ten youths have some positive foundation of morality.[62] After 50 years of working with aggressive children, Fritz Redl concluded that true child psychopaths are virtually nonexistent. Almost every child has some positive qualities. Redl proposed that somebody write a book titled *The Virtues of Delinquents*, but he speculated that it might be hard to find a publisher!

Pessimistic professionals seldom build powerful bonds with guarded young people, says delinquency expert Dr. Waln Brown. He describes his own background as a troubled child placed into alternative education schooling, correctional institutions, mental health resources, and residential treatment. He is extremely critical of many highly trained professionals who were assigned to help him with his problems. In time spent with his social worker, he recalls, "our eyes seldom met." Of his psychiatrist and psychologist, he says, "None of these professionals took the time to build even the slightest rapport or trust. If they had approached me in a less mechanical, more sympathetic manner, I might have provided them better insight."[63]

When children resist treatment, this is often seen as further proof of pathology. Some young people just do not make "good" patients but buck a therapist's attempts to change them. This could actually be seen as a potential strength since autonomy and self-determination are positively valued traits in our society.[64]

Too often, educators only see challenging students in terms of deficiencies. Simplistic curricula and pessimistic assessments betray a belief that these students probably don't have viable futures. Viewed through the pessimism lens, these students are defiant, disruptive, and disrespectful. Considering how effectively they manipulate our systems of behavioral controls, they might qualify for such labels as resourceful, resilient, creative, clever, and tenacious.[65] Educators who fail to see potential strengths beneath problems will be unable to redirect these students toward healthier goals.

Some educational and treatment programs neither educate nor treat—they make children worse. In medicine this is called an "iatrogenic effect." We spoke with a parent whose son had a difficult time in middle school because of Attention Deficit Hyperactivity Disorder (ADHD) and related learning problems. Then, when he was twelve and beginning puberty, they discovered he was involved in mutual sexual activities with his younger sister. They sought counseling help through the juvenile court. Their son was placed in a treatment program where he was sexually abused by other residents. He acted out more and again got into trouble. "When we finally got him back at age 17, he was damaged goods," his mother explained. "He had given up on school and had no vocational skills. Worst of all, he says counselors just stab him in the back, so now he won't trust anybody."

Our research on pitfalls of treatment for troubled students identified three common patterns of program failure.[66] The most
common abuse was when interventions deteriorated into coercion and intimidation. When students wouldn't comply, punishments, including physical restraint and isolation, were
inappropriately used. Sometimes staff allowed other students to
harass or punish their recalcitrant peers. A second common pit-
fall was depersonalized staff relationships. Treatment or teaching became empty rituals that blocked genuine communication.
Finally, some programs focused narrowly on a student's problems, failing to involve family and others in a child's life space
to create a partnership for change.

Karl Menninger is famous for his scathing attack on "the crime
of punishment." He was also highly critical of traditional treatment.[67] He once publicly "diagnosed" his psychiatric colleagues
with the disorder *furor therapeutics*; he said they were like sur-
geons who displayed a platter of bloody fragments of human tis-
sue and proclaimed that this is the result of surgery.[68] He called
for an emphasis on mental health rather than mental illness. He
was prophetic. We are now in the midst of a dramatic paradigm
shift that will rekindle the optimism of early youth pioneers.

Conclusion

One of the most enduring findings from delinquency research is
that approaches which are "repressive in character rather than
reconstructive" cannot succeed.[69] Educational and treatment
strategies for youth in conflict have been pessimistic and reactive. Attacking or discarding troubled youth are both failed
strategies. In the conventional view, punitive, get-tough
approaches are "conservative," while flaw-fixing rehabilitation is
"liberal." This is a false distinction. It is counterfeit conservatism
to discard our most difficult students. And there is nothing liberal
about patronizing young people as damaged or defective.[70]

A Detroit court sent 15-year-old Michael to Keweenaw, a profit-
making boot camp at an abandoned military base in a remote
region of Michigan's Upper Peninsula. Mike reacted with belligerence to demeaning treatment, so drill instructors tried to

make an example of him. They had the group harass him continuously. Peers held him upside down from a second story balcony and put him in a commercial dryer. Finally, during calisthenics they branded his back with an iron. Mike's severe burns brought the abuse into the open and the program was closed—for six weeks. Mike's rehabilitation took longer. When sent to our school, Mike was like a wild animal, hostile and fearful of adults and peers alike. A year later, as he prepared to return to the community, he described the contrast between the two approaches:[71]

> When I first came here, I fought staff when they corrected me. But when I got mad and disrespectful, instead of saying, "You can't talk to me like that," they listened, calmed me down and talked with me about my problems. I saw other kids who had courage to face their problems, and I wanted to change my life, too. Staff would tell us how much talent we have and they would stand by us even if we were in trouble. I am going home to finish high school, and I hope to someday get a degree and work with youth.

Michael returned to his community, and recently he told his former counselor that he is graduating from high school.

With the recognition that pessimistic approaches lead to a dead end, many are now calling for a course correction, where problems are seen as opportunities rather than threats. Resilience experts Sybil and Steven Wolin herald this new movement. They note that, traditionally, the fields of education, prevention, and treatment for youth in conflict have narrowly focused on risk. The results of this pessimistic approach have been disappointing. The most promising alternative to risk is the resilience model. This view honors the strengths of young people and nurtures their capacity to overcome hardship.[72] The following chapters describe how schools and communities are transforming problems into opportunities so that all children can thrive and flourish.

Works Cited

[1] Reprinted with permission from Children's Express. *Listen to Us!* 1978. New York: Workman Publishing. 19.

[2] Herman Saettler, a doctoral student in children's behavior disorders at the University of Illinois, compiled an extensive unpublished history of a century of abuse of children placed at the Chicago State Hospital.

[3] Woodward. 1999.

[4] Calhoun. 1998.

[5] Durkheim. 1972.

[6] Meade. 1918.

[7] Churchill is cited in Andre Ivanoff, Betty J. Blythe, and Tony Tripodi. 1994.

[8] Gilligan. 1997.

[9] Morgan. 1936.

[10] Reinharz. 1996.

[11] Regnery. 1986.

[12] Males. 1996.

[13] Allport. 1958.

[14] Barnao. 1999.

[15] Gordon. 1990.

[16] Larson and Brendtro. 2000.

[17] Jane Addams. 1909.

[18] Long. 1994. James Kauffman. 2000.

[19] Long. 1994.

[20] Murray. 1999.

[21] Fine. 1993.

[22] Fine. 1993.

[23] Garfinkel. 1998.

[24] Goodlad, Soder, and Sirotnik. 1993.

[25] Goldstein. 1999a.

[26] Kipnis. 1999.

[27] Hyman. 1997.

[28] Bush. 2001.

[29] Wood. 1995.

[30] Larson. 2000.

[31] Meade. 1918.

[32] Gilligan. 1982.

[33] Jones and Krisberg. 1994.

[34] Wylie. 1998.

[35] Amnesty International. 1998.

[36] Bishop, Frasier, Lonza-Kaduce, and Winner. 1996.

[37] Newsweek. 2000.

[38] Riak. 2001.

[39] Parks. 2000.

[40] Cooper. 1999.

[41] Ibid.

[42] Feld. 1999.

[43] Schwartz and Fishman. 1999.

[44] Brendtro and Cunningham. 1998.

[45] Kipnis. 1999.

[46] Reese. 1998.

[47] Cited by Amnesty International. 1998.

[48] Loeber and Farrington. 1999.

[49] Hale. 1997.

[50] Cothern. 2000.

[51] American Bar Association. 2000.

[52] Lewis et al. 1988.

[53] Amnesty International. 1998.

[54] Cothern. 2000. This is a study of practices surrounding juveniles, the death penalty, and life without parole. The council is headed by the attorney general and contains nine statutory members (federal department heads) and nine independent practitioner members appointed on a bipartisan basis by the Senate, House, and president. This report was an initiative of practitioner members rather than federal officials. Practitioner members were: Robert A. Babbidge, Jr., InterSouth, Inc.; Larry K. Brendtro, Reclaiming Youth International; Judge William Byers, South Carolina; John A. Calhoun, National Crime Prevention Council; Larry EchoHawk, Brigham Young University Law School; Judge Adele L. Grubbs, Georgia; Judge Gordon A. Martin, Jr., Massachusetts; Judge Michael W. McPhail, Mississippi; and Chief of Police Charles Sims, Mississippi.

[55] Goldstein. 1991.

[56] Hobbs. 1994.

[57] Raychaba. 1992.

[58] Wilson and Herrnstein. 1985.

[59] Wilson and Herrnstein. 1985.

[60] Kellerman. 1999.

[61] Kellerman. 1999.

[62] Gibbs, Potter, and Goldstein. 1995.

[63] Brown. 1983.

[64] Goldstein, Heller, and Sechrest. 1966.

[65] Cambone. 1994.

[66] We studied ten group treatment programs in a variety of settings from public and alternative schools to community based and residential group settings. In structured interviews with staff and students, pitfalls and abuses of programs were identified. This research was reported in Brendtro and Ness. 1982. For a further discussion of treatment failures, see Brendtro. 1995.

[67] Menninger. 1966.

[68] Gillogly. 1993. [69] Healy and Bronner. 1936.

[70] Brendtro and Ness. 1995.

[71] Personal communication, Terry Hood and Rod Ferguson, Starr Commonwealth, Albion, MI. September, 2000.

[72] Wolin and Wolin. 2000.

chapter three

Problems as Opportunity

Hate!
Hurt Enemies
War Battles Fights
People do show both.
Honesty Love Respect
Helping Friends
Care!

—Sarah, age 16[1]

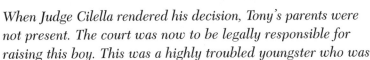

When Judge Cilella rendered his decision, Tony's parents were
not present. The court was now to be legally responsible for
raising this boy. This was a highly troubled youngster who was
a threat to his community. He was also still a child who was

failing in school and life. Over the years, Judge Cilella had sent other difficult youth who needed a fresh start to a school operated by Floyd Starr in Michigan. Tony needed to be removed from a destructive environment that placed him and others at risk. So, the judge ordered Tony to be placed at Starr Commonwealth to receive psychiatric therapy for fire setting.

Floyd Starr had known many fire-setters in his day. In 1915, the Chicago Daily News reported a speech that he gave before the local YMCA. He told the story of Ernest, a boy almost 13, who was an arsonist, tortured animals, and stole continuously. "The boy who burns down barns, lies, cheats, and disturbs his neighborhood isn't any different at heart from the boy who is held up in the same block as a model."[2] Many who spoke in court thought Ernest was a hopeless case and wanted him locked away in the state correctional school. Instead, the judge sent the boy to Starr Commonwealth. Ernest was to live in Gladsome Cottage, a two-story wooden structure. Mr. Starr gave the lad a tour of the house, pointing out where the money and valuables were kept. Then he put Ernest on his honor. The money was never stolen. Gladsome Cottage still stands.

But Floyd Starr was not naïve and knew that kindness alone was not enough. He taught his staff to balance trust with vigilance. Boys often slipped back into old ways and made mistakes. When trust was violated, this provided an excellent opportunity for character building. "Every bad boy is a potential good citizen," Starr told his 1915 Chicago audience. "Work, work, study, play, plenty of things to do and to think about—this is the curriculum of the commonwealth." Half a century later, another student who many saw as hopeless entered this Michigan school.

The court kept Tony locked in solitary confinement from January through March. While isolation was for his own protection, Tony felt bitterly abandoned. The detention facility became his private Alcatraz. He wanted to get out—but to be sent away from his family was to lose everything. He had never left his mother since she had refused to give him up at birth. But on a mid-April morning, Tony was loaded with his scant possessions to embark for Michigan.

The trip from Chicago to Michigan follows the course of Interstate 94. Driving south from the city, the highway turns toward Indiana. Smokestacks bellow a rusty stench from the foundries of Gary. After two hours of industrial sprawl, the highway opens onto the farms and orchards of southern Michigan. Watches are now set to eastern standard time. Halfway across southern Michigan, Starr Commonwealth looms ahead at exit 119. A large billboard displays an angelic lad heralding this as the place where "There is no such thing as a bad boy."

First impressions are disorienting. Could this possibly be a school for troubled students? The 350-acre campus with a pristine lake is surrounded by pine forests and farms. First laid out by a landscape architect, the campus rivaled any private boarding school in the nation. Floyd Starr believed that beauty is a silent teacher. Many boys came from lives of deprivation and ugliness. He would say, "I wanted to send them a clear message: This beautiful place is for you because you are of value."

Tony arrived at Starr Commonwealth in the afternoon. After school on a typical spring day, boys were busily engaged in a variety of work and recreation activities. Some rode in trucks toting tools for maintenance or farm workers. Others assigned to the grounds crew were fitted with boy-powered push mowers. They labored with laughter like a choreographed team. Mowing in flanks was more fun, and a group could cut a ten-foot swath through the expanses of bluegrass. From the band room in Webster Hall came the sounds of clarinets and trumpets blaring as the band practiced for Memorial Day. Other groups of boys would be fishing on the shores of Montcalm Lake or running on the track. Three months locked in a cell and now Tony entered a place without bars or fences.

Tony was officially supposed to receive therapy for fire setting. Remarkably, any reference to fires set by Tony had been purged from the records sent to Starr. It is unclear who made the decision to conceal Tony's past from his new caretakers. Treatment for fire setting certainly couldn't be arranged if this problem were not known. Was the court trying to lower the risk that Tony's past would become public? Possibly. Were the records sanitized to make admission more likely? Perhaps. But other factors were probably foremost in the judge's mind.

Judge Cilella realized that Tony needed more than talking to psychiatrists. This was an environment where a damaged boy could be restored to healthy maturity. As a juvenile judge, his task was to protect both Tony and the public. Following the original Cook County children's court charter, Judge Cilella would balance "the moral, emotional, mental, and physical welfare of the minor and the best interests of the community." By cleaning the slate, Tony was to be given a second chance. But it would not be so easy to purge a lifetime of pain and guilt from the mind of a troubled boy.

From Problems to Potential

I believe in chances, so I do not give up on people. . . . I believe in finding solutions to any and every problem.

—Ennis William Cosby[3]

Ennis William Cosby, son of entertainer and educator Bill Cosby and his wife Camille, was tragically murdered while stopped on a California freeway. Ennis had the ability to transform conflicts and problems into opportunities. As a bright sophomore in college, he sought testing to explore the reasons he was having trouble achieving. Ennis said that the happiest day of his life was when he found out he was dyslexic. "I believe that life is about finding solutions, and to me, the worst feeling in the world is confusion. I could not wait to find out about my strengths and weaknesses."[4]

Ennis graduated from Morehouse College and followed his dream to teach other young people with learning differences. He received a master's degree from Columbia and was pursuing a doctorate in education. A friend related an encounter between Ennis and children he met in a restaurant. When Ennis told them he was a teacher, the children shared the troubles they were having in school. After listening, Ennis suggested note-taking techniques and study habits he thought might help. He was literally teaching the children during dinner. Afterward, the children thanked Ennis and told him, "You really are a teacher." Ennis was simply doing what all teachers are pledged to do: give children the competence to surmount the challenges in their lives.

Citizens in Embryo

For over two centuries, pioneers in education and youth work have sought to reclaim challenging youth in environments rich in opportunities for love, education, work, play, and spiritual development. But this required adults who passionately believed in the potential for greatness in each young person.

After the Napoleonic wars, street children ran wild in major European cities. Johann Pestalozzi (1746–1827) gathered them into his castle school and sought to change them with love instead of punishment. He described these youth as filthy and vermin covered, ignorant, and arrogant. But he saw this as just the surface, for underneath were precious qualities waiting to be released. He concluded that punishment, unless carried out with great kindness, had contrary effects on troubled youth. He abolished flogging and declared that the crowning achievement of education was to be able to criticize a child's behavior in a spirit of kindness.[5]

The early twentieth century was an exciting time in the development of new strategies for troubled youth. The advent of democracy launched the radical ethic that children are more than property of adults. Everywhere, educators and child workers were breaking free from the coercive values that had marked patriarchal European civilization. Early education and youth work pioneers saw their mission as searching out strengths in the most challenging young people. Their optimism gave way to decades of preoccupation with deficit and deviance.

Now, once again, approaches to challenging youth are shifting from a pessimistic focus toward building potentials in all children and redeeming our most troubled youth.[6]

Janusz Korczak of Poland is perhaps the century's most renowned advocate for troubled children. He established a school for Jewish street children and authored the first of more than 20 books in 1901.[7] He worked with the juvenile court on difficult cases, including murder, but never lost his belief in the redeemability of youth. His life embodied the theme of one of his books, *The Child's Right to Respect*. Once Korczak criticized a noted doctor in a mental institution who had contended that youth in penal facilities lacked sensitivity. Korczak railed that it was a disgrace that a person with scientific training could write such a thing.[8] He demonstrated that these adolescents had the capacity for responsible self-governance. He decried the lack of respect shown by adults toward children and published a national youth newspaper to give voice to their views. Children are not *future* citizens he said, but *citizens in embryo*.

Austrian educator August Aichhorn presented his classic challenge to punishment in the book *Wayward Youth*.[9] At the time, the established approach to delinquent young people had been militaristic training. Aichhorn concluded that such depersonalized, punitive environments were destined to fail with "dissocial" youth. Although coercion might alter superficial behavior, he said, authentic character change required a strong identification with a prosocial adult, something Aichhorn saw as the primary unmet need of such children. He found that dissocial youth repeatedly exposed themselves to the danger of punishment. When educators inflicted punishment, they also became less attractive models for identification.

Maria Montessori of Italy developed programs for slum children that operated on the principle that true discipline was a noun—something children should possess—rather than a verb—something we do to children. She wrote passionately about their absorbent minds and created schools where punishment was replaced with inner discipline. She predicted that someday a museum to school slavery would be erected, and the prominent exhibits would be punishments and prizes—both designed to get students to engage in activities not meaningful to them.[10]

The leading pioneer to work with delinquent youth in Germany was Dr. Karl Wilker of Berlin. In 1917, Wilker was appointed director of Berlin's worst institution for delinquents, which incarcerated 300 boys under harsh, demeaning conditions. Wilker created totally new expectations for both staff and students. He demanded that adults learn to respect delinquent youth and that youth learn to take responsibility for their own behavior. Wilker created a children's court for self-governance, and when the time was right, the youth sawed off the bars of the now transformed facility. Wilker wrote a book on this experience titled after the name the students gave their school, *Der Lindenhof*. [11] This small volume became the rallying cry for the young people's empowerment movement of the Weimar Republic.

In South Africa, educator Alan Paton took over the worst delinquency institution of the apartheid era—Diepkloof—which held 500 black youth under the most primitive conditions imaginable.[12] Paton turned this into a model school and the success of his black students was an embarrassment to apartheid political leaders. His institution quickly became the center of political controversy. For a lifetime, Paton used the power of the pen to attack oppression, particularly of black youth. He is best known for his novel, *Cry, the Beloved Country*, which mobilized world opinion against apartheid.[13]

In the Soviet Union, the century's leading delinquency worker was Ukrainian Anton Makarenko; he created schools for youth who were terrorizing major cities. He founded his programs on the simple principles of work and joy. Makarenko was particularly harsh on the emerging professions that sought to "pathologize" the problems of disturbed youth. Given their defective relationships, their behavior was predictable. The notion that the problem resided in the child was a fixation of unsuccessful teachers and psychologists.[14]

Women prominently waved the banner of youth advocacy, even at a time when they didn't have the vote. In New Zealand, Sylvia Ashton-Warner defied the British educational system which was stifling aboriginal Maori children. She developed a revolutionary curriculum using experiential education and creativity as antidotes to aggression. Madame Song Ching Ling had a profound influence on education and child welfare in China. She said that schools should not just teach book knowledge but patriotism, globalism, respect for elders and the nation's history, and the ability and courage to recognize and fight against negative influence. In the United States, Jane Addams contended that a great deal of delinquent activities were the result of a misguided spirit of adventure, and her efforts gave rise to the first modern juvenile court in Chicago in 1899.

The early pioneers were courageous advocates for children who had been cast aside. Dorothea Dix began her work teaching Sunday school to delinquent girls. Before her work was finished, she sparked the mental health movement in both the U.S. and England. Elizabeth Sherrard saw the plight of Chicago street children and headed to Dakota to find them homes. She fearlessly stood against any person who dared to hurt a child. When a judge sent abused children back to a cruel father who horsewhipped them, she called a press conference to challenge the court. Sherrard castigated the judge and then announced to a startled press that she decided she had to train small children in the use of firearms. Therefore, when foolish judges put them in harm's way, the children would be able to defend themselves.

Barriers to Reform

These pioneers were powerful advocates of positive youth development. Unfortunately, the programs they began usually declined with the passing of the founder. They had the right idea but were ahead of their times. They lacked three crucial elements to support their proposed reforms: (1) a *receptive political climate*; (2) a *science of positive child development*; and (3) a *system for training workers* to ensure program integrity.

Education and juvenile work reformers encountered powerful political resistance. Most espoused strongly democratic philosophies in cultures that were still very authoritarian. Maria Montessori was mocked. Janusz Korczak of Poland was executed. Sylvia Ashton-Warner was fired by colonial authorities, and her creative curriculum was destroyed. When Hitler came to power, Karl Wilker's writings were ordered burned by the Nazi regime, and he fled to South Africa to escape execution. In that nation, Alan Paton initiated similar reforms but was toppled by the forces of apartheid. Paton described the frustrations of reformers everywhere: "I shudder at the thought of a corrupting society that punishes and even kills those it corrupts."[15]

Early youth pioneers operated without a science of prevention and intervention. These were dynamic and charismatic individuals who created programs in the shadow of their own personal philosophies. Most had a flare for the dramatic and spontaneously improvised strategies and solutions. Following the Russian Revolution, Anton Makarenko taught street urchins and was proud that he operated on gut instinct rather than grand design: "I am still in a stage of searching and becoming. . . . What I have to tell you are rather intuitions than conclusions."[16] Of course, it might have been possible to turn intuitions into testable hypotheses. But the pioneers were totally engrossed in the face-to-face needs of their students and preoccupied with the survival of their programs. Thus, a great gulf developed between theory and practice. Educators and youth workers didn't have time or training to conduct research. Researchers studied topics of little relevance to those working with tough kids.

Youth pioneers lacked effective ways of teaching their methods to others. In a classic study of delinquency, researchers Eleanor Glueck and Sheldon Glueck concluded that, "The best of systems must fail if those who do the work are not adequately equipped in attitude and training."[17] Without a professional and scientific knowledge base, success depended on acquiring practiced wisdom over a lifetime of experiences. While several pioneers wrote about their work, they usually dealt more with philosophy than technique. The main way of gaining expertise was to become an apprentice or understudy. This kept successful ideas from spreading very far beyond a particular program or pioneer. Further, just following around behind a master did not provide the novice with a road map to similar competence. Most understudies were less gifted than their mentors and much practiced wisdom was buried with the founder.

Today, critics dismiss these reformers as quaint, naive "child-savers." We are told that today's violent youth are "different," since delinquency in earlier times was little more than Sunday school children throwing spit-wads. In fact, these pioneers worked in times when problems were overwhelming and resources were almost nonexistent. They were no strangers to violent youth or to children sexually abused in depraved homes. Teens ran lawless on the streets, and children were locked in jails and savaged by adult criminals. Children had easy access to drugs and guns. Nevertheless, these pioneers were not discouraged but turned adversity into advantage. They saw their troubled young charges as their greatest asset, and certainly worth reclaiming.

Back to the Future

Goethe once declared that the job of the educator was to find the germ of virtue concealed in the kernel of every fault. This spirit gave rise to democracy in education, the child guidance movement, and courts for juveniles. But this progressive era gave way to deficit-based models in education, psychology, and juvenile justice. It was as if for a time, professionals became so overwhelmed by the problems of children that they lost sight of their potentials. There are now cracks in the pessimism lens as strength-based approaches experience a robust revival.

Resilience expert Waln Brown concludes that the fields of mental health and juvenile justice have been remiss in their analysis of human potential:

> One is left with the impression that most, if not the majority, of young people who exhibit pronounced behavior problems are destined to a lifetime of adjustment difficulties. Institutionalized children

would seem beyond hope. Nothing could be further from the truth. . . . Valuable insights are lacking with regard to how children who currently exhibit behavioral problems might be helped to facilitate a prosocial behavioral change.[18]

The past need not predict the future. New relationships, opportunities, even random events can change the path of one's life.[19] Resilience studies have identified the factors that enable persons to overcome adversity. This is leading to a new approach to intervention based on cultivating strengths. Perhaps we can change the odds in knowing how some high-risk youths and families can surmount them.[20] Strength-based perspectives shift our attention toward a developmental, rather than a pathological view of the lives of troubled youth. The focus becomes providing the supports and skills that permit a youth to meet his or her own needs and surmount life's difficulties.

Reflecting on their 30-year study of Hawaiian youth, resilience researchers Emmy Werner and Ruth Smith conclude, "If we encourage and nurture these dispositions and competencies in our children as best we can, we have a basic survival kit for meeting adversities that tax the human spirit."[21] They contend that a more optimistic perspective makes us aware of the self-righting tendencies of children who are progressing toward normal adult development, even under adverse circumstances.

The strength-based model is experiencing a revival among education, mental health, justice, and child development professionals. Eric Laursen defines strength-based intervention as supporting and reinforcing child and family assets rather than focusing on individual or family deficits. The educator or helping practitioner takes on the role of a partner rather than an expert.[22] Even when working with very seriously troubled students, strength-based methods are showing promising outcomes.[23] Methods of assessment are also being transformed in order to identify not only problems but potentials.[24]

Modern research validates what was long known by pioneers who worked with troubled youth. Given opportunities, young people can surmount even the most difficult backgrounds. This philosophy is now being rediscovered and applied to reclaiming discarded youth. Zvi Levy of Israel operates Youth Aliyah schools for uprooted youth. He suggests that it is more effective to help youth build an optimistic future than to soothe past distresses. These youth need hope from adults in their lives: "The message is: What is inside you is good enough to take you to places you have never dared to go."[25]

Environments of Respect

A youth must be respected. How do you know that his future may not exceed your present?

—Confucius—551–497 B.C. [26]

Adults in every school and community bear responsibility for building environments in which children and adolescents can thrive and grow. Peter Benson calls this the *youth development infrastructure*. But in virtually any community, a typical youth receives less than half of the *developmental assets* associated with healthy outcomes. Ironically, troubled youth most needing positive support are being discarded.[27]

While there is much discussion about positive adolescent development, this concept has not been clearly defined. A promising approach to positive youth development is the CCDO resilience model first described by John Seita, Martin Mitchell, and Christi Tobin.[28] Healthy outcomes result from environments that provide *connections, continuity, dignity,* and *opportunity*. Here we define CCDO and give examples of the presence and absence of these crucial factors.

❑ **Connections:** Support and guidance through strong, positive relationships.

Without at least one person who cares, youth cannot develop full potential.

❑ **Continuity:** Events and pathways that shape one's life story.

Some young people are locked in patterns of failure and broken relationships.

❑ **Dignity:** The development of self-worth in a climate of respect.

There is no dignity in residing in environments of despair and gloom.

❑ **Opportunity:** Positive environments that foster growth and change.

Without external support, inner strength, and positive goals, youth cannot thrive.

CCDO applies to a full range of settings including education, juvenile justice, treatment, and family and community-based youth development. These principles are relevant in childhood, adolescence, and the transition to adulthood. We summarize this model of positive youth development.[29]

Connections

Human beings are born into this little span of life of which the best is its friendships and intimacies.

—William James[30]

Adolescents receive nurturance and social controls through positive bonding to family, peers, schools, and community.[31] In an unhealthy ecology, youth are weakly bonded to the people and institutions of society. Social bonding motivates individuals to live in harmony with the standards of the group to which one belongs. Strong connections have been shown to prevent a wide variety of high-risk behaviors, including precocious sexuality,

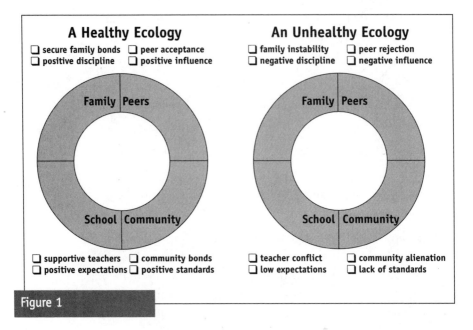

A Healthy Ecology
- ❏ secure family bonds   ❏ peer acceptance
- ❏ positive discipline   ❏ positive influence

Family | Peers

School | Community

- ❏ supportive teachers   ❏ community bonds
- ❏ positive expectations   ❏ positive standards

An Unhealthy Ecology
- ❏ family instability   ❏ peer rejection
- ❏ negative discipline   ❏ negative influence

Family | Peers

School | Community

- ❏ teacher conflict   ❏ community alienation
- ❏ low expectations   ❏ lack of standards

Figure 1

school problems, violence, delinquency, and drug abuse.[32] For healthy development, Urie Bronfenbrenner contends that each child should have at least one person who is irrationally crazy about him or her.

Ideally, children are reared in environments offering rich opportunities for connections to positive adults and peers. When one area of the ecology is unstable, such as the family, other support systems can enable youth to thrive. Throughout most human history, the tribe and extended family provided necessary social support to all children in a kinship network. Today, the challenge facing fractured families and communities is to create new support systems so that all children can succeed.

In the two centuries since Johann Pestalozzi gathered street urchins into farms and castles, environmental treatment has been the most enduring intervention for wayward adolescents.

Dr. Nicholas Hobbs developed a successful model for changing troubled behavior by surrounding the young person with a positive ecology. This program was called Re-ED, an acronym for the Re-education of Emotionally Disturbed Children. Hobbs trained his teacher-counselors to create environments for growth using core principles, which are summarized below.[33]

Trust is the glue that holds teaching and learning together. The first step is to teach young people that adults can be predictable sources of support, understanding, and affection. No amount of professional training can make an adult worthy of the trust of a child or capable of generating it. A child should know some joy in each day. We do not retreat and try to repair the past. Each new day is an important opportunity to start anew. No one waits for a special therapeutic hour; the goal is to make all hours special. We teach youth to look beyond present problems to the challenge of a positive future.

Children can become competent, and school is the natural support for helping children in trouble. They gain new skills and learn about their behavior and relationships with others. Engaging young people in learning achievement brings many satisfactions and strengthens students' perceptions of worth. Positive feelings should be nurtured through creative activities and the joy of companionship. Challenging physical activities are important because the body image is integral with a person's self-identity. Education is an adventure in which children can test themselves and learn to master the fear of failure.

The group is very important to young people. In a positive group, it is difficult for young people to behave in disturbing ways. Even when the group is functioning poorly, planning activities and surmounting difficulties is a maturing experience. Group ceremonies and rituals create order and comradeship. Many children come from families detached from community. Children must develop positive links to communities. By participating in community projects, they widen their horizons and build new goals for their futures. In all of these normal educational processes, time is an ally and adults are there to support the normal restorative process of growth.

Continuity

The psychologist acts here like a novelist who has to construct a human being with a definite line of action, style of life, or pattern of behavior.

—Alfred Adler[34]

Alfred Adler got to know children by constructing lifelines to discover how their current behavior might be anchored in past experiences. We use the term *timelines* to describe the patterns of behavior that lead youth to follow certain life pathways. Adler noted that the specifics of what happens to a person in life are not as crucial as the private logic that a person holds about these events.

Every young person has an intense need to tell his or her story. As we listen, we learn how a young person deals with real-life problems. Adults can offer their support by helping a young person clarify and solve problems. In this process, we come to understand motives and needs behind a child's behavior. Even students with learning and intellectual disabilities can provide rich details about their experiences, if this can be explored as an oral story.[35]

Behavioral psychologists try to determine the purpose of behavior with a "functional assessment" by studying a timeline sequence called ABC, which stands for *Antecedents, Behavior,* and *Consequences.* Timelines can be of short duration, like a single behavioral incident. Other important timelines cover longer periods, such as trajectories of violence or sequences of placements. Following are key behavioral timelines that are important to track.

Behavioral incident timelines provide a helpful teaching tool because our students often don't think in a logical, sequential fashion. For example, an adolescent says, "The teacher kicked me out of class because he is a jerk." Timelines help students to check their logic against reality and acquire a valid perspective on their behavior. Students can also learn to identify common thinking errors.[36]

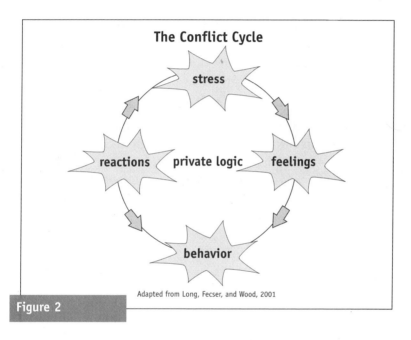

The Conflict Cycle

stress

reactions private logic feelings

behavior

Adapted from Long, Fecser, and Wood, 2001

Figure 2

Conflict cycles are behavior incident timelines mapped in a circular pathway. This cycle demonstrates how conflict escalates. Stress triggers feelings, such as anger. These feelings then drive behavior. Some people react to this behavior, often in ways that increase stress. When a person is overwhelmed by stress, they are in a crisis. They don't have coping strategies for facing this challenge. By examining conflict cycles, one can discover the way a youth copes with life challenges.

Problem pathways cover time periods longer than a single incident. They offer a picture of behavior patterns and trends.

Sometimes, minor problems can grow more serious and they become entrenched lifestyles.[37] For example, we can chart the decline in frequency of a problem behavior across a school year. An even broader calendar might track the ages at which a young person experienced particular problems. With students who have been bounced around, a timeline of changes in placements can be useful. In peer-helping groups, the "life story" shared by members provides a way of scanning important life events and identifying coping strategies.

When we understand a child's characteristic way of thinking, feeling, and behaving, we are in a better position to teach and guide that youth. Unlike the typical behavioral incident report that focuses on offense and punishment, the timeline shows how patterns of self-defeating behavior develop.

In general, we help students focus on present and future rather than the past. But sometimes one has to revisit the past before getting on with one's future. In discussing problems, we are careful not to communicate that we are hunting for pathology. Rather, we are seeking how the person copes with difficult situations in life. However destructive their early environment, we want students to develop survivor's pride instead of seeing themselves as "damaged goods."[38]

Dignity

The market value of the very young is small. Only in the sight of God and the Law is the apple blossom worth as much as the apple, green shoots as much as a field of ripe corn.

—Janusz Korczak [39]

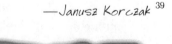

Throughout much of European history, children were classified as property, and abuse was rampant. In contrast, many tribal cultures revered their young. The Lakota word for child is literally translated as sacred being: One would never strike or shout at one who was sacred. The Maori term describing a child is "gift of the gods." A Zulu professor of sociology notes that in his African tribe, the child is the embodiment of positive spiritual values:

> The mere sight of a child touches the very essence of our humanity. A child draws from within us the inclination and instinct for kindness, gentleness, generosity, and love. Accordingly, there is nothing more revolting to our humanity than cruelty to children. These truths we knew at one time and, somehow, subsequently forgot.[40]

Dignity is fostered in environments that teach values of respect. Children who grow up devalued and disrespected internalize the message that they are worthless. In order to develop social responsibility, youth must have opportunities to become involved in helping and caring for others.[41] But as one girl said, "It's very hard to care for others when I don't even care for myself."

How can we help children develop self-worth and a sense of personal dignity? Stanley Coopersmith conducted extensive research on how children form ideas about their value as people. He found that youth measure their self-worth against these four benchmarks:

1. Significance: "Am I important to somebody?"

2. Competence: "Am I good at something?"

3. Power: "Can I influence my world?"

4. Virtue: "Am I a good person?"

Youth vary in the importance they attach to each of these factors, but all four benchmarks contribute to the development of a sense of self-worth. Self-esteem is not related to physical attractiveness and only weakly correlates to social status, material wealth, and academic performance.

Self-worth is more than superficial self-esteem. There has been much legitimate criticism about the pop-psych movement, which offers quick fixes to hype self-esteem.[42] Psychiatrist David Burns promises that ten days of self-esteem therapy will snap you out of depression and will reveal the secret joys of living.[43] We recall attending a large conference where a self-esteem "trainer" instructed all 600 of us in the audience to shout, "I am great!" Then we were to give the nearest stranger a shoulder massage and tell the person how great he or she is. Self-esteem is not feel-good narcissism.

Coopersmith outlined specific ways adults can nurture self-worth in children. Children develop *significance* through the attention and affection of others. Effective caregivers provide the child with acceptance without overprotection and discipline without rejection. Children develop *competence* as they experience the joy of achievement. Effective caregivers provide positive expectations and opportunities to be creative and to explore, offering encouragement in times of failure. Children need to develop a sense of their own *power* to be able to influence others and control their destiny. As effective caregivers set limits with respect, youth gain confidence and learn to cope with adversity. Finally, children develop a sense of *virtue* as they embrace positive values. Effective caregivers are not permissive or uninvolved but set standards of conduct that children internalize.

The perspectives of science are balanced by the voice of youth in this appeal by seventh-grader Jerome His Law from the Pine Ridge Indian Reservation:

> I want to be treated with respect and dignity. If you
> respect me, I will respect you. If you take pride in
> me, I will take pride in you. But if you treat me bad
> I will probably abuse myself by drugs, alcohol, and
> low self-esteem. This is going to all the parents on
> earth. Give us love and attention, listen to us when
> we have a problem, and talk to us when you have a
> problem. Because when you ignore us, it makes us
> feel stupid and mad. It feels bad when we get hurt
> by bad names, teasing, taunting, and being ignored.

So, talk it over with somebody, and tell your kids you love them.[44]

Opportunity

To reclaim is to restore dignity to young persons who have been devalued, to cultivate courage in environments of belonging, Mastery, Independence, and Generosity.

—Martin Brokenleg

Long before modern science, First Nations people of North America raised children in environments providing rich opportunity for healthy growth and development. They used sophisticated educational strategies designed to nurture caring, respectful, and courageous children. We have called this child-rearing philosophy the Circle of Courage, as depicted by Lakota artist George Blue Bird. (See Figure 3.)

There is strong evidence that the Circle of Courage values apply across time and culture. Unlike other models for education, these concepts do not come from theory or research, but from the traditions and practices of cultures that deeply cherish children and treat them with respect and dignity.

European domination was calculated to decimate the cultural traditions of tribal peoples. Fueled by the doctrine of divine destiny, the motto of colonial education was "Kill the Indian to save the child." Children who had never experienced force with anger from an adult were ripped from their families and sent to boarding schools where they were beaten if they spoke their native tongue. Similar practices occurred on all continents where Europeans colonized indigenous peoples. Aboriginal Australians call the victims of this cultural kidnapping "The Stolen Generation." Europeans sincerely believed they were civilizing savage children. But the Europeans actually had primitive theories of child development, believing children were evil and needed to be beaten into submission. In contrast, many tribal nations had sophisticated child-rearing systems designed to teach courage instead of obedience.

The Circle of Courage embodies four core principles for nurturing all children in a climate of respect and dignity cited by Larry Brendtro, Martin Brokenleg, and Steve Van Bockern.[45]

1. **Belonging:** The universal longing for human bonds is nurtured by relationships of trust so that the child can say, "I am loved."

2. **Mastery:** The child's inborn thirst for learning is nurtured; learning to cope with the world, the child can say, "I can succeed."

3. **Independence:** The child's free will is nurtured by increased responsibility so that the child can say, "I am in charge of my life."

4. **Generosity:** The child's character is nurtured by concern for others so that the child can say, "I have a purpose for my life."

Child-rearing customs vary in different cultures and families, but the developmental needs of children are universal. When children are deprived of these four essentials, they become discouraged and defiant. Environments that fail to provide belonging, mastery, independence, and generosity are toxic to children.

The Circle of Courage is both simple and profound. Young children can understand its concepts. Researchers see it as a practical synthesis of knowledge about positive youth development.

A model demonstration school in Utah employs a behavioral curriculum based on the science and technology of direct instruction. Viewed through the eyes of children, the goals of their school are portrayed on a window painted with the Circle of

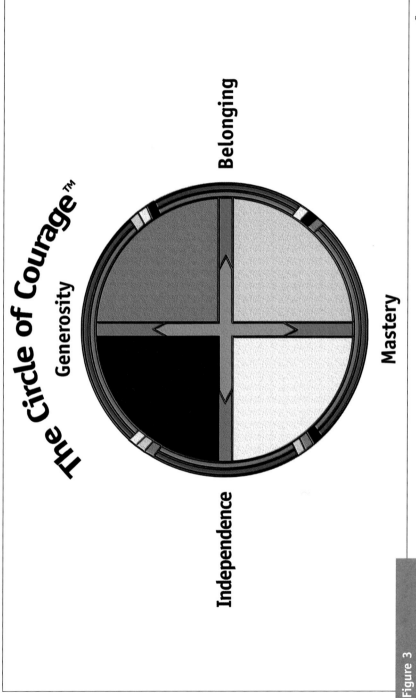

The Circle of Courage™

Generosity

Belonging

Independence

Mastery

Figure 3

Art by George Blue Bird is reproduced with permission of Circle of Courage, Inc.

Courage. Surrounding the circle are colored palm prints of students. Beside each is a small note of encouragement. The reinforcers are tailored for each child describing how the student has displayed belonging, mastery, independence, or generosity.

Cathann Kress of Cornell University worked with the National 4-H organization using the Circle of Courage to address problems of violence and racial conflict. A project called VOICES was implemented in a racially troubled school. Students learned to transform conflict into community. Sixteen-year-old Noy was part of this project: "I've learned to take part in my community and lend a hand. We also develop skills. We learned how to try to make someone see our side without being aggressive or passive."[46]

While training staff at a Vermont high school, we first met with students at risk. They had painted the Circle of Courage on the wall of their group meeting room. Sitting in a circle, students shared the ways their circles were "broken" as well as things they were doing to develop belonging, mastery, independence, and generosity in their school. Later we had a meeting with the principal and her faculty. One teacher observed, "Many of us have been talking about how we need to work on our own circles if we are to teach these values to students. Instead of showing belonging and generosity, this faculty fights for turf. We need more skills to become master teachers. And, we are at war with administration and don't feel empowered as professionals." They spent the next two hours rebuilding their relationships with one another and their leadership team.

In British Columbia, a second-grade teacher hung a Circle of Courage poster on the wall as a constant reminder to her students. One child was so eager to give the right answers to everything that he constantly crowded other students out of class discussion. The teacher took him aside to explain that she was pleased he wanted to participate but that he wasn't giving others a chance to tell what they know. "Oh, now I get it," the boy exclaimed. "It's a generosity thing!"

Rebellion as Resilience

If the child persists in activities we do not like, we dub him obstinate, stubborn, 'hardboiled', perverse, unruly or headstrong. If he persists in actions which please us, we speak of him as determined, strong-willed, resolute, brave, unflinching."

—John J. B. Morgan[47]

However dysfunctional a child's behavior seems, it usually is a goal-directed attempt to meet some basic needs. Alfred Adler was among the first to note that children who fight others may be signaling strong unmet needs for human belonging. Maria Montessori even heralded such aggressive youth as admirable, because at least they were fighting against an unfair world instead of giving up as was the case with passive youth. In our more modern times, professionals assign them deficit and disorder labels and then try to fix their flaws.

For some time we have been training—perhaps we should say retraining—education and treatment professionals to focus on the capacities of youth, rather than just on their weaknesses. Our colleagues usually are quite surprised that by reframing their perceptions, they rapidly increase possible treatment interventions. Patterns of troublesome behavior can suggest previously unrecognized strengths or areas where competence can be further developed. Following is a case in which we were asked to discuss Rodney, who was presenting extreme behavioral problems.

The Boy in the Drug Business

Rodney is a small, wiry, 14-year-old African American who was sent to a private treatment center for highly aggressive behavior. In spite of normal intelligence, he was failing in school. His files contained a diagnosis of oppositional and conduct disorders. Rodney had been experiencing conflict in school for several years, but he became increasingly uncontrollable after his father died from heart failure related to crack use.

It was rumored that Rodney had served as a lookout for his father, who was in the drug business. Rodney was the only one present when his father died, and he tried in vain to revive him. Rodney's mother has a debilitating handicap, and she abuses the use of medications given to her for her condition. She is often unable to tend to the younger children, and their care falls to Rodney, who is the oldest child. At other times, Rodney hung out in the streets without supervision.

In the treatment center, Rodney provoked fights with peers, used inappropriate language, and sought to be the center of attention in class by clowning and talking back to teachers. When challenged, he was totally defiant to adult authority and accused the staff of being racist, which is a significant issue because almost all the staff are white.

Rodney resisted all attempts at counseling, in spite of the fact that his father's death had been very traumatic. He had told a peer that he was to blame because if he had studied CPR better in school, his father would still be alive.

Treatment and educational interventions should be based on an evaluation of the youth's needs. Following the Circle of Courage model, humans normally pursue the goals of belonging, mastery, independence, and generosity.[48] When the Circle of Courage is broken, children display patterns of personal and social maladjustment. Instead of belonging, children display alienation. Without mastery, children feel incompetent and are frustrated by failure. Children who have not gained independence are irresponsible. Lacking generosity, young people live lives that are selfish and purposeless.

Applying the Circle of Courage model to the case of Rodney, we see that his basic needs have been unmet and his behaviors reflect this.

Belonging: Rodney's alienation from staff signals problems with relationships. With the death of his father, he lacks any strong bonds with adults and he seeks other antisocial youth for substitute feelings of belonging.

Mastery: Rodney fails in school, but his competence on the street is well developed. School problems are probably related to his antagonism toward authority figures, rather than the absence of ability.

Independence: While Rodney fights all efforts of others to control him, he also acts in irresponsible ways that suggest a sense of powerlessness and a lack of secure independence. Children not securely attached have great difficulty becoming securely independent.

Generosity: The loyalty and support Rodney showed to his disabled mother and drug-abusing father, and his concern for his younger siblings, show a clear sense of empathy.

As seen above, both adaptive and negative behaviors often are cut from the same cloth. Normal explanations for problem behavior, when plausible, are preferable to pathological explanations.

Discovering Potentials Beneath Problems

In searching for explanations for behavior, we are less like diagnosticians and more like *suspecticians*, to borrow a term coined by Eli Bower.[49] Our job, like scientists, is to be suspicious of unproven suppositions. As we raise questions, we are able to form alternative hypotheses, and then see whether our theories hold water. When we abandon deficit views and study Rodney's behavior more closely, we see there is a certain logic to his behavior. A number of positive potentials are lurking beneath his problem behavior.

Why is this youth aggressive? The conventional wisdom is that aggressive students have flaws in their personality or character. However, staff concluded that Rodney had learned to be combative as a street survival skill. It is his gutsy demeanor rather than his small size that must be his protection. He communicates by verbal and nonverbal means, saying that no one better mess with him or he will attack anyone, regardless of size. Only when he comes to feel safe will he be able to abandon the tough-guy role. Hostile staff response only fuels his fighting spirit. Rodney could benefit from understanding the conflict cycle, which traps him into escalating interactions where he sees no option but to save face by fighting. With trust, he should be able to discuss what he is trying to prove with his fighting and re-evaluate whether this combative role is necessary in his current environment.

A close examination of incidents of aggression showed that Rodney only fought staff or boys his own size or bigger (that is, those who presented a challenge). Here is a selectively aggressive youth who does not use his power to bully weaker people. This shows both self-control and a sense of protective concern for others. His apparent empathy for children may be related to his role of protecting younger siblings at home. Staff felt this suggested the possibility for using these strengths, by placing him in a responsible role with younger students.

Much of Rodney's aggression is verbal. He seems to be "playing the dozens" in a kind of verbal insult game, which is entertaining on the streets, but disruptive in school or his residence. Most white staff get very upset at his street jive and gestures, which probably is as much their problem as it is his. Ideally, a culturally sensitive staff would be best able to handle this particular situation. It was suggested that the staff read *Ribbin' Jivin' and Playin' the Dozens*, so they will feel more competent when faced by his street games.[50] Since he is very clever with his verbal wit, he undoubtedly is more intelligent than is shown by his school performance.

Why does this youth resist relationships? The conventional wisdom is that students like Rodney are incapable of forming positive attachments. Certainly, Rodney is quick to attribute hostile intent to others and is thin-skinned about any challenge to his reputation. Staff concluded that this pattern of distrust is not a "thinking error." In his private logic, this makes perfect sense, given his experiences to date. This world-view might have made sense on the mean streets where one must constantly be on guard to protect oneself against trouble. In school, such distrust actually produces more trouble.

Rodney is particularly resistant to counseling. He says he doesn't need a "shrink," so he may think counseling suggests craziness or weakness. However, his refusal to play the patient role may telegraph more strength than weakness. Likewise, his apparent guilt about his father's death is a sign of normality. He blames himself for not being able to revive his father with CPR; this suggests he sees himself as the only responsible party in a family with two irresponsible parents. While it is important for him to get past self-blame, this is further evidence of his concern for others.

Staff will need to look for naturally occurring situations that provide opportunities to help Rodney question whether his distrust of others is valid. Trust for Rodney may be particularly hard to establish with the mostly white staff. There are, however, some opportunities for developing attachments to an African American mentor who could provide a positive male role model for Rodney. This is crucial, as there are relatively few black role models in the agency. Initially, trust is built primarily through positive activities. Once having shown some goodwill during a time of crisis, the staff can draw on this trust and help Rodney rethink his view of others as enemies.

Rodney had positive attachments to both his father and mother in spite of their problems, and he willingly helped them with the "business" of drug pushing and child care. He is a youth capable of building bonds to significant others. It is unlikely his mother can meet his needs for adult affection and guidance. Thus, he needs other opportunities to attach with a prosocial adult. He may also need to distance himself emotionally from the problems of his mother. However, it would be a mistake to assume that she has no strengths, since she certainly has succeeded at building loyalty in her oldest son. Rodney will respond best to natural counseling about practical problems. This will allow him to form a partnership with an adult in shared problem solving. As he discovers that adults are not punishing and they refuse to get trapped in power struggles with him, he should be able to develop positive relationships with them.

Why is this student failing in school? The conventional wisdom is that a student like Rodney lacks motivation. But beneath all of his problems, we see an intelligent youth who uses his wit and will to challenge others and to keep people at bay. His problems with aggression and guarded relationships directly contribute to school failure. Teachers must tap his positive strengths and build an alliance with him.

Rodney's desire to interact with peers suggests he might do better in a classroom designed around cooperative learning. Since his only close relationships at present are with peers, it would be a mistake to try to shove him into a study carrel to keep him under control. A positive bond with a teacher should increase the likelihood that he will become meaningfully involved in learning.

Attention-seeking behavior should be treated as an attempt to communicate, rather than as a challenge to authority. An acting activity might spark his interest, as he could then legitimately be the center of attraction. Attempts need to be made to inspire him to think of possible future career interests, then revolve the curriculum around those interests (or subjects). Rodney's strong sense of humor can signify a way to building healthy attachments. Also, a more multicultural classroom would reduce the alienation between schooling and life. When Rodney decides school can help him achieve something of importance, his strong will and verbal skills should be decided advantages.

The staff initially asked to discuss Rodney because of their frustrations that nothing was working; the only alternatives seemed to be more intrusive consequences leading to his removal from the program. The strength-based mindset called on them to switch to a problem-solving mode. Staff were able to brainstorm and opportunities for positive interventions opened up immensely.

Developmental Audits with Difficult Students

The Developmental Audit™ offers a new approach to educational and treatment planning with challenging students. When an airplane crashes, a careful study is made of all of the factors contributing to the disaster, so preventative steps may be taken. When a kid crashes, we just build a thicker file documenting failure. Some young people sabotage all efforts to help them. Clearly they do not benefit from the usual discipline or consequences. The Developmental Audit is designed for such students.

The Developmental Audit uses interviews to understand conflicts in a child's life in order to determine why a young person chooses to engage in self-defeating behavior. It is used with students whose chronic or serious problems place them at risk for removal from school or placement in restrictive settings. The Developmental Audit is also used for functional assessments required in special education as well as in treatment planning in mental health and juvenile justice cases.[51]

The Developmental Audit follows the CCDO format. *Connections* to family, school, peers, and community are identified. This shows what support systems are available or needed. *Continuity* of behavior is studied by exploring timelines of significant events to determine the meaning behind the behavior. These patterns of thinking and coping influence life pathways. This establishes the goal or function of behavior and identifies coping strengths and problems. *Dignity* is related to a student's sense of self-worth and respect for others. *Opportunity* is the interventions plan to foster growth and change. The final Developmental Audit report tells the story of the young person and answers the important questions: How did this young person come to this point in his or her life? Where can we go from here?

The first Developmental Audit was conducted with a young adolescent who had wounded other students in a gun incident, sparked by school bullying. Based on the audit, the court ordered a period of detention, followed by placement at Father Flanagan's Boys Town. The boy thrived and graduated. When he left for college, he told his adult mentors, "You gave me a name instead of a number."

An example of a Developmental Audit was featured on the CBS *Sixty Minutes II* news program, "Three Year Nightmare."[52] Dean was a bright student with ADHD and Tourette's Syndrome (involuntary tics and uncontrollable verbalization including obscene language). He encountered continual frustration and peer harassment in school. Dean developed oppositional behavior, began using alcohol, and was involved in minor delinquency. He was placed under court supervision and sent to a juvenile facility. For three years, Dean coursed through boot camps and youth prisons. Instead of tapping his strengths, authorities became locked in escalating conflict with Dean. Abused by staff, his behavior deteriorated, and he became self-destructive. He and peers were being locked in isolation cells 23 hours a day for weeks at a time without any education or treatment. When the boys created a disturbance in their cellblock, they were transferred to an adult prison and charged with felonies. Dean's judge asked Reclaiming Youth International to conduct a Developmental Audit. With this comprehensive assessment of Dean's problems and strengths, the courts were finally able to make an informed arrangement. The judge criticized the state for mishandling these boys, removed Dean from prison, and enrolled him in a residential school to receive the education and treatment he needed.

The Developmental Audit provides a new standard for planning interventions when youth face life-altering decisions in schools, courts, and treatment programs. With a clear understanding about the real nature of problems and strengths of a student, we are better able to create opportunities to help these young people reclaim themselves.[53]

Conclusion

When adults are in adversarial relationships with students, both sides employ strategies to attack, avoid, or outwit the other. If young people are clever enough to sabotage our educational efforts, they are mature enough to be involved in building positive school communities. When youth become partners in their own education and healing, they no longer use their considerable talents in rebellion and defiance.

By enlisting the resources of youth, we create a climate of mutual respect. Problems can be approached either as opportunities or as threats. Operating from threat, the question is, "What consequences can we impose to stop this student's defiant behavior?" This strategy leads us down the slippery slope of punishment, exclusion, and/or manipulation. From a problem-solving mindset, we ask, "Why does this student continue defiance in spite of recurrent consequences?"

In searching for opportunity, we discover strengths and engage in a problem-solving process. The most promising interventions reframe problems as opportunities. The Resolving Conflict Creatively Program teaches students respect and problem solving. Peer programs enlist youth in the hopes of caring for one another. The Girls and Boys Town Teaching-Family model gives students relationship skills and empowers them with self-control. Life Space Crisis Intervention helps youth explore timelines of problems to change self-defeating thinking and behavior.[54] All such strategies draw youth into respectful problem-solving alliances with adults.

Works Cited

[1] Poetry from a student at Woodland Hills, Duluth, Minnesota, published in *Reclaiming Children and Youth*, 5(2):107.

[2] Starr. 1915.

[3] Ennis William Cosby. 1998. *Teaching from the heart*. Hello Friend/Ennis William Cosby Foundation. www.hellofriend.org

[4] Drs. William H. and Camille O. Cosby established The Hello Friend/Ennis William Cosby Foundation to fulfill the goals and dreams of their son. Ennis's common greeting, "Hello Friend," inspired the name of the foundation, which is dedicated to celebrating the gifts and

potentials of people with dyslexia and language-based learning differences. For more information on the foundation or to meet Ennis in his own words, see the Web site www.hellofriend.org.

[5] Kilpatrick, 1951.

[6] Krisberg and Austin. 1993.

[7] Korczak. 1967.

[8] Korczak. 1929.

[9] Aichhorn. 1935.

[10] Montessori. 1967.

[11] Wilker. 1921/1993.

[12] Alexander. 1994.

[13] Paton. 1948.

[14] Rose Edwards. 1994.

[15] Alan Paton. 1986.

[16] Edwards. 1994.

[17] Glueck and Glueck.

[18] Brown. 1988.

[19] Bandura. 1982.

[20] Furstenberg, Cook, Eccles, Elder, and Sameroff. 1999.

[21] Werner and Smith. 1992.

[22] Laursen. 2000.

[23] Marquoit and Dobbins. 1998.

[24] Epstein. 1998.

[25] Levy. 1993.

[26] Confucius. In Arthur Waley. 1938.

[27] Benson. 1997.

[28] Seita, Mitchell, and Tobin. 1996.

[29] Mitchell, Barrett, and Seita. 1998.

[30] William James cited in John Cook (ed.) 1996.

[31] Bronfenbrenner. 1979.

[32] Haggerty and Garmezy. 1994.

[33] Hobbs. 1994.

[34] Adler, 1932.

[35] Baker and Gersten. 2000.

[36] Gibbs, Potter, Goldstein, and Brendtro. 1998.

[37] Loeber and Farrington. 1998.

[38] Wolin and Wolin. 1993.

[39] Korczak. 1967.

[40] Vilakazi. 1993.

[41] Brendtro and Ness. 1983.

[42] Hewitt. 1998.

[43] Burns. 1993.

[44] His Law. 1993.

[45] Brendtro, Brokenleg, and Van Bockern. 1990.

[46] Kress and Forrest. 2000.

[47] Morgan. 1936.

[48] Brendtro, Brokenleg, and Van Bockern. 1990.

[49] Bower. 1960.

[50] Foster. 1986.

[51] Developmental Audits are conducted by a team headed by an individual with specific competency in Life Space Crisis Intervention and Developmental Audits. In addition to observation and case records, a key data source is the youth and others in his or her life. Using Life Space Crisis Intervention interview methods, the Developmental Audit tracks the young person's pathway to trouble.

[52] CBS. 2001.

[53] Training and certification in the Developmental Audit is provided by the nonprofit organization, Reclaiming Youth International. For more information, write Reclaiming Youth International, Augustana College, Sioux Falls, SD 57197, or refer to its Web site, www.reclaiming.com The Developmental Audit is trademark protected by RYI.

[54] Long, Fecser, and Brendtro. 1998.

Building Strengths

Glance at problems, gaze at strengths.

—Jamie C. Chambers[1]

Like all new boys, Tony was assigned to a residence on the main campus. He was welcomed by the other youth, but living in a house with a dozen other boys was scary for a lad who had spent most of his life without siblings or friends. Huge Tudor-style houses built between the world wars made the campus look like a fashionable suburb.

It was awkward for Tony to hear the other boys call the houseparents "Mom" and "Pop." They weren't his parents. They were strict, but the other boys didn't seem afraid of them. The boys were responsible for keeping the cottages spotlessly clean. Tony's name was added to the chart on the wall for chores. Setting tables, serving, washing dishes, carrying garbage, mopping bathrooms—all of these chores were part of a system that seemed strange to Tony. A favorite job was being a buffer boy: With polishing pads under their feet, boys skated around polishing hardwood floors to a high shine. The boys had to keep their lockers and beds in perfect condition. Tony was given the small handbook with tips on cleanliness and good manners. The most important rule was that selfishness was off-limits. As Floyd Starr would say, "Commonwealth means we all share in common every good thing that happens."

School was held in three buildings situated near the lake. Students switched classes like on a college campus. One building housed academics, another vocational, music, and art programs, and the third was a fully-equipped gymnasium near the sports field. Tony wasn't strong, but he would be toughened with rigorous daily physical education. After school, play alternated with hard work. More competitive boys elected sports, while those who were less athletic, like Tony, signed up for the band.

The campus had a natural rhythm of events calculated to provide structure and strengthen character. In the spring, boys planted gardens and trees. Floyd would tell the boys, "Every year we plant new trees to replace those that will be lost to lightning, wind, or disease." He would then show them the tree planted by Helen Keller on her visit. He said it was a privilege to help plant trees because the boys were giving a gift to future generations of students.

The school schedule was reduced in summer, as recreation and work became prominent. There was perpetual weed pulling and lawn mowing. Much activity centered around Lake Montcalm with its swimming beach, boats, and canoes. Every holiday was celebrated. The Fourth of July might even bring the governor of Michigan landing in his helicopter on the school's athletic field. The Boy Scout troop was in high gear preparing for camping excursions.

In September, it was back to school and football. All eyes were now on the first Sunday in October, Founders Day. Every year, a famous speaker such as athlete Jesse Owens or poet Carl Sandburg would draw thousands of visitors. All cottages and classes were open for tours. The boys baked cookies and, as tour *guides, hosted guests. Founder's Day was when alumni returned. Floyd Starr enjoyed showing his "old boys" off to the current crop of seedlings at his "character farm." Here were youth role models who had overcome adversity.*

In autumn, crimson maple and golden oak leaves carpeted the lawns. The boys who mowed were replaced by raking brigades. Halloween was time to bring in the produce from the gardens. As Thanksgiving approached, boys would hear the story of the first "Fast Day" in 1913. It seems a street youth from Detroit started the tradition by asking if he could skip a meal so the cost could help starving friends of his in Detroit. The other boys joined him in the fast and a tradition was established. For decades, Mr. Starr would retell the story. Then with great drama, he would proclaim that no boy had ever refused to give up a meal for some starving brother out there. He would then call for them to raise their hands if they wanted to continue the unbroken chain of generosity. The vote was always unanimous.

At Christmas, fire was an important symbolic ritual. There was always a candlelight chapel service where all the light came from the candles each boy held. The highlight of the season was the "Little Builder of Christmas Fires" ceremony. All would gather around a huge fireplace built into the gymnasium wall just for this annual event. Floyd Starr would sit in a rocker by the fireplace and read the story of a boy who brought firewood to warm loveless homes. Then, the smallest boy in the Commonwealth would have the honor of lighting a match to the stack of wood in the fireplace. According to tradition, if there was enough love in the Commonwealth, the fire would light with only one match. To ensure a roaring fire, Mr. Starr would have the maintenance department presoak the wood with kerosene. It was the biggest legal blaze that most had ever enjoyed.

Nobody seemed to have more energy than Floyd Starr. He was everywhere on the campus and would pop up unannounced in classrooms or residences anytime, day or night. Delinquents are awed by power and here was a man who had his own community named after him. New students always followed the cue of the veterans who rose to their feet and greeted Mr. Starr whenever

Chapter Four Building Strengths

he entered a room. Often he would go around the group giving each boy a handshake. New boys with averted gazes or limp grips were yanked back with a hearty smile and encouraged to try it again with vigor. This was Social Skills 101. Visitors were always amazed that these former delinquents could meet strangers with more confidence and charm than privileged children. Meals also had to be conducted with grace and etiquette. While most boys didn't like it, they had to wear ties to dinner. Floyd repeatedly explained to his students the reason for good manners: "I want any of you boys to be able to eat with Henry Ford, someday." He had great expectations.

Every Sunday, boys walked with their staff to the Chapel in the Woods. Presiding was a jolly giant of an Anglican priest, Father Austin Pellet. For boys who had family visits, chapel was the highlight of the week since parents would meet them there. For boys who didn't get visits, the sight of parents in chapel triggered feelings of abandonment. To compensate, Father Pellett pumped out the message that every boy belonged in the family of God.

At some chapel services the founder himself gave the sermon. He preferred to call these little talks "Golden Moments." Now nearing eighty, Uncle Floyd's homilies mostly recalled boys from the early years who had made good. He repeated the same stories so many times, most boys and staff soon knew them by heart. One of his all-time favorites was the same one he had told at the Chicago YMCA in 1915—about Ernest, the boy who stole, burned barns, and drowned chickens. Like most Golden Moments, this story had a happy ending. The so-called bad boy many thought was hopeless was selected as the outstanding boy at the State Sunday School Convention. Good overcomes evil.

All the boys knew the Starr Commonwealth Creed for it was posted and proclaimed everywhere. It began with the declaration that every boy will be good if given an environment of love and activity. The activity part was easy in this beehive of work, study, and play. But boys like Tony import painful experiences and private logic that convince them they are unworthy of love. "Why should I trust these people?" Tony was starving for love, but he kept to himself.

Belonging: Powerful Alliances

*If you succeed in gaining their love,
. . . it will be in your power to direct
them into almost any path you choose.*

—Samuel Hall, 1829[2]

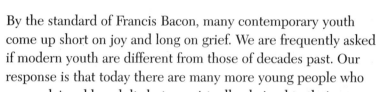

By the standard of Francis Bacon, many contemporary youth come up short on joy and long on grief. We are frequently asked if modern youth are different from those of decades past. Our response is that today there are many more young people who are unclaimed by adults but are virtually chained to their peers. When adults give up on youth, cultural values are no longer passed on by elders but are relegated to peers.

Bonds between people are communicated by claiming behaviors. These are signs that mark who belongs and who is an outsider.[3] For example, one might use a kinship term or nicknames to signal friendship. Physical signs such as clothing, tattoos, and gang identifiers can also signal belonging. Ceremonies and rituals are used to induct a person into a group, honor achievements, and manage separation as a celebration. Distinctive schools are rich with such traditions. In building positive environments, one can creatively institute such traditions.

Michael Williams, as director of the Hannah Neil Center for young troubled children in Columbus, invented a "Hannah Neil Handshake." As hokey as it sounds, the adolescents loved it as they flocked around him waiting for their greeting. A summer camp in the western United States climaxes each session with a rodeo where every rider is a winner. Then, as all the young wranglers sit on the corral fence, the camp director gallops his horse down the fence line, giving farewell high fives to all with outstretched hands. At the Black Hills Children's Home, special

ceremonies are used to say farewell to students who are depart-
ing, complete with stories, lighting of candles, and refrains of
"friends are friends forever."

A critical factor in socializing children is to replace disruption
with engagement. Adults who engage youth foster trust, build
self-worth, and offer positive models. Unfortunately, many conflicts and disruptions alienate children from adults. This leads to
noncompliant behavior and further contamination of relationships.[4] This downward spiral of maladaptive behavior must be
reversed by new experiences and unions. It is essential to build
positive bonds with youth and to repair ruptures in relationships.

A positive relationship has been described as the red thread
that runs through all effective helping interventions.[5] This concept was a dominant theme in early education and youth work
programs. Then, competing notions of "professional distance"
and "boundaries" began to put caregivers and troubled kids at
arm's length. Many former youth in care have written powerful
critiques of this philosophy of detachment.[6] Keeping a distance
from students is not supported by research. For example, some
assume that creating dependency interferes with self-reliance.
In fact, the most independent youth are those who have been
securely connected to caring adults. Some believe youth prefer
to develop close ties to peers instead of adults. Youth want
peers for friends but don't trust their advice; they want guidance from a wise adult whom they trust. Some contend that
social distance is necessary for maintaining authority. In reality,
youth are much more responsive to adults they like than those
about whom they couldn't care less.

Research on effective helping shows that relationships are more
powerful than technique. Half or more of the successful outcomes in many treatment studies can be attributed to an
"alliance" between the mentor and the person being helped.
This is also true of teaching. Yet, instead of an alliance, many
youth and adults are in hostile encounters as shown below.[7]

Distrustful youth are skillful in resisting relationships with the
helping adult. Adolescents erect barriers to communication so
they are unable to learn from adults. They don't respond to the

The Hostile Encounter	The Respectful Alliance
Distrust—The young person does not believes this adult genuinely cares, understands, or is able to help.	**Trust**—The young person believes the adult genuinely cares, understands, and is able to help.
Antagonism—Young person and adult work at cross-purposes. Typically the adult seeks control and the student wants autonomy.	**Collaboration**—Young person and adult work toward common goals as they join forces in problem solving and positive growth.
Detachment—Mutual hostility increases avoidance and social distance.	**Engagement**—Mutual respect increases communication and social bonding.

adult as a social reinforcer so they are indifferent to criticism or praise. Finally, they reject adult models and become prisoners of peers.[8]

Building trust with relationship-resistant students is an endurance event. For example, once a youth starts to form an attachment, he or she may need to temporarily test the adult's commitment by an act of purposeful defiance. One student skipped several appointments with his new mentor just to see if the adult would give up on him. A person who cannot decode this behavior will not connect to such individuals.[9] Even after a bond has been built, there will be times when conflicts erupt. The adult is responsible for preventing relationship meltdown.

The helping alliance between adult and child is part of a broader set of relationships which are essential to successful outcomes.[10] Children need close connections within family, school, and peer group. Adults sharing responsibility for a child also need to work as a team. These interlocking relationships can either create a climate of conflict or cooperation.

Peer Group Relationships

All young people need to learn from peers and other adults beyond their immediate family. This allows them to transcend the flaws of their parents, gain new skills and perspectives, and of course, become independent.[11] However, all parents are concerned that their children might fall into the wrong crowd. Fortunately, most adolescents select friends who are compatible with their values and family background. Others join with peers who support them in rebellion against adult authority and values. Even moral giants such as St. Augustine and St. Francis of Assisi ran with delinquent gangs in their youth.[12]

Any school or group setting must deal with the reality of a youth subculture. A negative peer climate will undercut the most sophisticated programs. Large depersonalized schools mass-produce negative cliques and subcultures. Strong adult-youth bonds alone cannot eliminate a negative youth subculture since it largely operates underground. Often, those in authority wage war against negative peer cultures by trying to identify negative leaders and punish or remove them.

Dramatic changes occur when youngsters abandon conflict with adults or competition with one another to become a cohesive, prosocial group. Peer helping can have a profound impact on students who would be scapegoated in other settings:

> Laurel was an overweight teenager, had poor hygiene, and wouldn't let people become close to her. When participating in an obstacle course, she wanted to give up; she did not want to risk embarrassment. Her peers told her they would not go on without her, so they literally carried her up over the barriers. They traded off like geese in formation so no one would be overwhelmed by the difficulty in encouraging her. "I am not going on. Leave me!" she would say. But they kept her with the group, until in a miracle of exertion, they got her over the barrier. It is hard to say whether she or her peers were more jubilant at their accomplishment.

this is a picture of me all by my self

Art by Melissa

In a culturally diverse society, positive peer groups must create
acceptance across racial boundaries. Trevor was biracial; his
father was black and his mother was white. He didn't want
peers to know about his mother because he was embarrassed
about her and he was very angry, asking, "Where do I belong?"
When he shared this with peers, they embraced him. Later, he
was able to develop skills as a mediator with children from different racial backgrounds.

Once we learn how to create cooperative peer group relationships, we come face to face with the troubling inconsistency

Chapter Four Building Strengths

that *adults have not learned to work together in a true spirit of teamwork!* Nothing could be more unsettling than a cohesive group of troubled youth confronting a disjointed, chaotic staff. Thus we come to another necessary condition for successful re-education—in other words, effective teamwork relationships among adults.

Teamwork Relationships

In spite of abundant rhetoric on the importance of collaboration, many schools and youth agencies are marked by "organizational bedlam."[13] Professional jargon, turf-tending, staff feuds, layers of middle management, remote administrators—all of these work against teamwork. In the words of Bill Morse, the various professionals conspire to chop up the child into little pieces so that each might have a share. Many professionals spend much time in conferences and meetings, but this does not equate with teamwork.

If we really believe in teamwork, then we must quit talking about it and make it a real priority. We call this *teamwork primacy*. This means that building strong staff teams becomes the foremost administrative goal. Teamwork primacy starts by assigning each staff member to a team that has specific responsibility for a certain group of students. Then, like any effective sports team, regular meetings are needed to develop and implement the "game plan." Schedules may need to be rearranged to enable maximum participation by all program staff in team meetings. It is important that the staff remain on a close par with the students (or with one another) to generate creative ideas. All team members must be involved in decisions that affect the program for students. Finally, all team members help develop the skills of fellow team members.[14]

Research shows that negative staff groups that lack cohesion create negative peer climates,[15] which can lead to greater conflict in the youth group. When staff are coercive, youth will more likely victimize their peers. If staff have pessimistic views of youth, young people will distrust them. Finally, if the staff inflicts punishment, a no-narcing code between the students conceals problems.

Positive staff teams produce positive youth groups. When staff treat youth with respect and autonomy, delinquent values in the group decrease. When there is a problem-solving focus, even disturbed and troubled youth improve in functioning. Staff who instill great expectations for success foster a student culture with greater interest in school. Students who develop close bonds with the staff are more able to seek adult support and guidance from other adults in their lives.

Educators need to collaborate with parents and other professionals in order to create environments that meet the complex needs of many students. The narrow academic focus of schools has meant that children with special mental health needs have not been well served. Most school districts have no capacity to provide sophisticated counseling services themselves. Zina Steinberg calls for greater infusion of psychologists and social workers who would work side by side with teachers in observing children, understanding behavior, and developing interventions. Crisis management should be woven into the fabric of the school so students in trouble will experience "time in" instead of "time out." For example, schools provide more support to students instead of throwing them out, and on-site clinicians serve as case managers to coordinate planning with other agencies, linking home with school.[16]

Some schools discard children they cannot serve, while others enrich programs for these same youth. The Alberta Safe and Caring Schools legislation in Canada brought both youth care workers and police into schools. Schools in California and Minnesota have become the base of operations for youth probation staff and child mental health teams. The most revolutionary model for bringing health and social services to students and families is the "full service schools" movement. In the past, agencies working on problems of sex, drugs, violence, and stress were scattered, duplicated, and uncoordinated. Increasingly, current health, mental health, and social service agencies are establishing programs in schools. In the long run this is a cost-effective way of creating powerful environments that support children and families with whatever they need to "make it."[17]

The basic error is to suppose that a person's will must necessarily be broken before it can obey. Were this reasoning to be applied to intellectual education, we should have to destroy a person's mind before we could give him any knowledge.

—Maria Montesorri[18]

One of the first educators to specialize in difficult students was Maria Montessori. She opened schools for children from the poor sections of Rome and discovered they had remarkably "absorbent minds." Montessori was particularly drawn to students who challenged adult authority since she felt they had more inner strengths than students who were passively obedient. The key to success with these reluctant students was to recognize their hidden creative talents and engage them in tasks that could capture their concentration.

While many educators are pessimistic about students from difficult family backgrounds, schools often have more profound impact on these students than with privileged children. Although these students enter school with many problems that interfere with school performance, once they are engaged in learning, the results are remarkable. Even if their family problems cannot be solved, schools give every youth a daily opportunity for success, responsibility, and positive attention. Dirk is an example of such a student. Coming from a turbulent family and school background, he moved to a new community where teachers gave him a fresh start. He shared, "I feel I belong and most everyone has been very supportive of me. I feel as though I have many friends, not just students, but teachers also."

John Odney enlisted high school students in grading their schools.[19] Listening to voices of youth, he found striking contrasts in how schools could impact students for better or worse. A bright senior student described the failure of his close friend, Ray. Ray was having a particularly hard time in his life and his problem snowballed in school; then he began to get behind in his work. The accumulating make-ups led to in-school suspension. Ray's friend said, "All the pressure kept building up and after 11 1/2 years of school, he dropped out. I know it was because of the make-ups and ISS (In School Suspension). It was hard for me because we have been best friends since second grade. Now I am about to go off to college, and he's still looking for a job."

When students are able to connect to teachers, school can become an island in a stormy life. Michelle was very upbeat about how school contributed to her positive growth: "Most of the faculty here make an effort to get to know you. It really makes me feel like I belong when a teacher calls me by my first name even when I am not in their class. We have a wide spectrum of students, and everybody has at least one friend and they aren't always from the same socioeconomic background."

Safe and Reclaiming Schools

An ounce of prevention is worth a pound of metal detectors.

—Linda Lantieri[20]

Linda Lantieri and Educators for Social Responsibility launched a movement for safe and peaceable schools after the shooting death of a New York City principal.[21] Lantieri contends that our ability to turn our schools into caring communities rather than armed fortresses will determine the future of our young people. This will require teaching students the value of respect and the skills for managing conflict. Educators can use naturally occurring discipline problems as a curriculum for nonviolence. Conflict becomes an opportunity for teaching skills in creative resolution. Such programs are not frills. Students must be able to resolve conflicts with peers and authority problems with adults.

Successful schools provide a climate in which all students can thrive. We conceptualize this as a three-level pyramid. At the base is *Primary Intervention* which means providing opportunities for all students to achieve. Next is *Early Intervention* for students whose backgrounds or behaviors make them vulnerable. Finally, a small group of students who display serious learning and behavior problems need *Intensive Intervention.*

Primary Intervention includes rich academic and social curricula and positive discipline systems. Direct instruction, literacy training, cooperative learning, and experiential education will enhance academic success. Socioemotional competence comes from building character, social skills, respect, empathy, and racial harmony. Positive discipline teaches conflict resolution and builds a positive student climate. For example, *Discipline with Dignity* provides educators with the skills to manage problems in respectful ways.[22] *Bully-Proofing Schools* programs mobilize a caring majority of students to defuse the power of bullies and support vulnerable peers.[23]

Early Intervention focuses on students who need additional support. Families from high-risk neighborhoods receive parenting courses and their children are given social skills training. Such programs reduce aggression and increase bonding to family and school across elementary grades.[24] Systematic screening instruments are available to identify students who may be at risk for developing behavior disorders.[25] Many students only pose problems part-time and can succeed if they have access to counseling or crisis intervention at times of duress. *The Tough*

Kid series provides practical management strategies and social skills for success with challenging students.[26]

Intensive Intervention focuses on more difficult students who have very high needs. They require comprehensive approaches that may involve agencies outside of the school. Functional assessments are used to identify the purpose of their behavior. A rich array of research-tested methods are available for use with challenging students.[27]

The *Safe and Civil Schools* program developed by Randy Sprick of the University of Oregon addresses all three levels of the pyramid. This comprehensive school-wide approach strives to build environments that are both safe and humane.[28] Dr. Sprick describes his approach as proactive, positive, and instructional. Proactive means getting ahead of the problems rather than merely reacting. Positive means that all staff are respectful and every student receives more recognition for responsible behavior than for misbehavior. Instructional means the staff teach expectations, and if problems arise, they correct and re-teach.

Safe and Civil Schools begin by creating a unified school policy so the staff can act with consistency. Another component is giving each teacher an effective management plan for the classroom that fits his or her instructional style. Staff examine the total school setting to prevent problems in classrooms, halls, the cafeteria, and on the bus. The goal is to build emotional and physical safety instead of narrowly focusing on violence or weapons issues. A variety of materials and training opportunities develop positive discipline in classrooms and throughout the school culture. These interventions have been found to reduce behavior disruptions and disciplinary referrals, improve attendance, and increase staff satisfaction.

All school staff need skills to succeed with difficult students. They are confronted daily with stress and conflict, and their armor can wear thin. Students in conflict stir up normal feelings of counter-aggression in adults. Those not trained to understand and manage these feelings react with hostility and escalate conflict into crisis in order to enhance the "holding power" of teachers.

The Safe and Reclaiming Schools program was developed by Nicholas Long of the Life Space Crisis Intervention Institute.[29] The focus is on building positive communication with students and using problems and crises as teaching opportunities. This comprehensive program also follows the three-tier pyramid model.

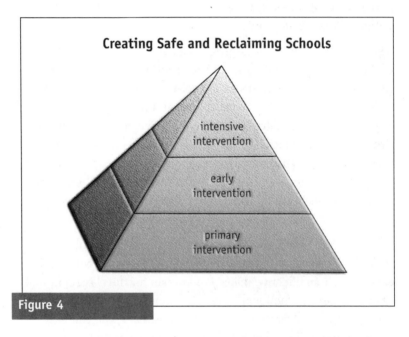

Creating Safe and Reclaiming Schools

intensive intervention

early intervention

primary intervention

Figure 4

Primary Intervention training is provided for the total school staff. They learn to recognize conflict cycles and use skills in anger management and stress reduction. Other skills help them create a predictable environment where rules and structure are administered without hostility. Staff learn specific surface management techniques to maintain positive student behavior. They practice skills of positive talk, decoding the meaning of behavior, and affirming student feelings and behavior.

Early Intervention training provides classroom teachers skills for success with four types of students: aggressive, passive-aggressive, depressed, and anxious-withdrawn. Staff identify "carry-in problems" that start outside the school, de-escalate crises, and connect students needing additional help to the crisis reclaiming team.

Intensive Intervention is coordinated by the school's Crisis Reclaiming Team. At each site, two or more staff serve on this team. Membership might include a counselor, social worker or psychologist, a special educator, an at-risk coordinator, or a school administrator. Team members receive an advanced five-day experiential certification course in Life Space Crisis Intervention.[30] This includes research-validated competencies for engaging and problem solving with students who present any of these six patterns of problems:

1. Students who import home or community problems to school

2. Students who distort reality and blame others for their problems

3. Students who bully or misuse other students without apparent regret

4. Students with low self-worth who berate themselves for normal mistakes

5. Students who are socially rejected and lack positive social skills

6. Students who are vulnerable to negative peer influence

With a comprehensive school-based program and a stimulating curriculum, most students can succeed in mainstream educational settings. Still, the needs of some will best be addressed in small, intensively staffed alternative settings. These personalized settings can create positive experiences and relationships with students whose disruptive behavior is at a level of severity not tolerable in normal settings.

Alternatives for Success

Alternative schools that segregate challenging students have proliferated in spite of calls for inclusion. Students with emotional or learning disabilities are the first to be sent to alternative settings. Some programs are little more than curriculums of control.[31] Other alternatives have a rich creative curriculum and a range of mental health services.

Starr Commonwealth operates various alternative schools for day and residential students. These offer individualized instruction, counseling, a positive peer climate, and parental involvement. Individualized academic programs follow a diagnostic-prescriptive methodology in academic skills. Transition programs offer life skills, such as prevocational training and independent living. Community resources for experiential and outdoor education are extensively used. Service-learning captures the interest of many students. Mark, a student, was enthusiastic: "We give back what we took in community service. We adopt a family and give them meals, and learn responsibility."

Counselors work closely with teachers, who also see themselves as teacher-counselors. Roles are flexible and all staff join in activities beyond the traditional instruction, such as camping. Many students enter with the attitude of "I hate teachers." They soon discover an intimacy neither typical nor encouraged in public schools. Through field trips, parent contacts, and close interpersonal relationships, staff communicate commitment beyond the call of duty. Maria, who is a student, explains, "Teachers take time to sit down, talk with you, and help you to be more interested in school. In public school they just gave me an assignment and there were no 'redos' if it was wrong."

Alternative schools achieve structure without rigidity. In large organizations, controls are imposed by elaborate rules instead of primary-group human relationships. Cross-age grouping, varied courses, and spontaneous access to the community create a highly stimulating and challenging climate. The staff builds a common spirit within the alternative school while helping students focus on future placement in another school, vocational training, or employment. A typical student stays one or two years, since the goal is to return to the traditional setting.

Strong involvement of families is a hallmark of the alternative school. Staff engage parents as partners, based upon the uncommon notion that we need them at least as much as they need us. The staff does not presume that the problems of the young adult are necessarily of the parent's doing—most parents feel this responsibility regardless. Family counseling and support groups are available if needed, and parents are seen as partners.

Alternative schools employ ongoing evaluation including attendance and behavior measures, achievement testing, and consumer (i.e., students and their families) evaluations. The typical high school student enters with reading and math achievement four years below grade level. Average reading achievement increases from a grade level of about 6.5 at admission pretest to 8.0 at the end of a nine-month academic year. The reading gain of 1.5 grade levels in a year is twice the rate of the student's past history. Once behavior is not an issue, full attention can be given to learning. Said a student named Ron, "We concentrate here and get more work done. In public school, we wasted time."

Absenteeism from previous high schools was 25 percent compared with six percent in the alternative school. Parents expressed strong satisfaction, with 86 percent rating alternative school staff as understanding their problems and needs to a "great extent" or "very great extent." Virtually none of the parents rated prior schools that their child attended in these categories. Students feel safe and secure in an educational alternative environment. A student named LaMar put this in concrete terms: "Here you don't get shot like my cousin who was 17. You can't skip school, either."

Walking through an Albion, Michigan, alternative school with director Dr. Herman McCall, we met Jamie, who was disruptive and rarely attended his old school. He was with two other students: Sarido, who was kicked out for carrying pepper spray and Terry, who threatened peers with weapons. All are on the honor roll. They go to school when the rest of the district is having snow days. One walks three miles if his parents can't bring him. We asked the boys, "What advice could you give teachers to succeed with kids like you?" They told us that ISS didn't work and they just got further behind. They described helping other students as a peer listener. All three agreed that whatever happens, staff will help them work it out. "They care about us here. In my old school, they wanted to get rid of me," Terry elaborated.

Some students who succeed in alternative programs, drop out after returning to public school, according to McCall. He investigated the reasons for these failures by following students from alternative school into regular school and comparing those who succeeded with those who dropped out. In the opinion of mainstream school teachers, "poor parenting" and "poor student attitude and attendance" led to dropping out. The students themselves cited "poor treatment" by the school as their main reason for dropping out, in other words, the school "had an attitude" about them. Less common reasons some students dropped out were peer influence and to seek employment. McCall concluded that students who succeed in alternative schooling only to later drop out have greater needs for individual attention and supportive teacher-relationships than are forthcoming in mainstream schools. He proposes that alternative schools help mainstream educators develop skills for dealing with these students. Along with that, students should have the opportunity to return to alternative school rather than drop out.[32]

Martin Gold found that school success is a powerful contributor to positive outcomes for students at risk. "Such youth are notorious for their poor attendance and performance at school. Their failure to live up to the demands of the student role is a major trigger for their antisocial behavior. When they have some success at school, then their misbehavior subsides."[33] Mike , a student, put it this way: "People think a school like this must be violent. In my last school kids were fighting all the time. Here we have few fights. We have more responsibility. Just like college."

Independence: The Road to Self-Reliance

Ours is a culture where youth are excluded from responsible participation only to be blamed for their irresponsibility and belligerence.

—Ruth Benedict[34]

A founder of American public education, Horace Mann (1796–1859), declared that the purpose of schools in a democracy was to provide an "apprenticeship in responsibility." By the beginning of the twentieth century, schools and youth programs were transformed from authoritarian to democratic philosophies. Adult coercion and intimidation was replaced with young adult self-governance. Even difficult students were treated as citizens-in-training. Schools were renamed as republics, villages, commonwealths, and boys' towns.

Self-Governance

In a 1927 law school dissertation, Cora Liepmann of Germany surveyed youth governance programs for "wayward youth" in Europe and the United States. These programs worked to greatly reduce the animosity between young people and adults, and they permeated obedience models in education. Students were taught a sense of *community responsibility*. Then, procedures were designed to involve youth in *self-governance*. Finally, youth were educated in providing *mutual help* in their peer groups.[35]

A century later, programs of youth participation are being revived as young people join with adults to transform their schools and youth organizations. The National Peer Helpers Association operates a large network of supportive services initiated by peers in schools, churches, and community settings.[36] Thousands of other models involve young people in substance-abuse education, dropout prevention, suicide awareness, health promotion, gang-prevention, bully-proofing schools, and conflict resolution.

Effective models of youth work enlist young people as partners in developing a positive learning environment. In the Girls and Boys Town "empowerment model," students help set rules. Aggression Research Training groups teach social and self-management skills to create the "prosocial gang." The most intensive use of peer groups are in peer-helping programs such as EQUIP or Positive Peer Culture (PPC) where youth are empowered as partners in their own healing.[37]

Many barriers prevent access of young people to participate responsibly in a team setting. As with other cases of prejudice, those students who are subdued are "kept in their place" by stereotypes and rationalizations used by those in power. These rationalizations are similar to the earlier debates about whether women or blacks should be allowed to vote. Larry Brendtro and Joan Bacon discuss a number of these myths and misconceptions:

> Youth wouldn't understand what's happening and don't have the ability to contribute. They are still immature and don't know what's best for them. Those in charge can tell them about it later. Having everybody participate is inefficient. A few knowledgeable persons can decide what is best. Besides, students would only manipulate to get their way.[38]

Canadian researchers asked youth in out-of-home placement about their involvement in planning their futures. Not one out of 36 young people had been involved in designing their case plan. They conveyed feelings of helplessness in the face of adults who controlled their lives. Such youth are unlikely to be willing participants in plans cooked up by adults. Youth have definite opinions about their futures and will share these views if given encouragement and the opportunity.[39]

There are successful examples of involving youngsters as team members in planning their futures. Some schools and youth organizations are arranging places on governing boards for youth. A state task force studying gang problems had significant representation by teenagers from varied backgrounds. In Canada, a National Youth in Care Network was formed to give adolescents who had been in the care system a voice in planning student policies and programs.[40] The group has even provided testimony before legislative bodies. These are voices seldom heard by policy makers.

If students are to be involved in planning their futures, problems must be put into perspective by focusing on strengths and goals. As a student, Jenny had a long history of psychiatric and school difficulties. She had been in a special education alternative program for a year, and the school was adopting a new policy to involve youth in their IEP (Individualized Education Program) meetings. It was determined that her past history of school failures and psychiatric hospitalizations would not be rehashed. The starting point for the conference was that Jenny had made it through a school year without needing hospitalization. Jenny expressed concerns about a mainstream algebra course that she failed. Her ideas were taken seriously and adjustments were considered. The team frankly shared their view that Jenny tended to exaggerate the significance of her failures. She accepted this criticism in a new climate of cooperation. Later recalling that successful IEP conference, Jenny exclaimed, "I've never seen my mom beam before. My parents were so satisfied that they took me to McDonald's."[41]

Transition to Independence

The road to responsible adulthood is difficult, even with a supportive family. When young people first attempt independence, they need to be able to learn from failures. If problems recur, this offers the opportunity to strengthen coping strategies or teach new skills. When young people lack a stable family, communities need to support them in their transition to adulthood. Faith-based organizations are sleeping giants in this regard because they can embrace youth in a caring community. Vocational, educational, and counseling resources also inspire students toward positive goals.

Santino was 16 and had no family. He entered a Starr Independent Living Program in Detroit after previous placements for delinquent behavior. Counselors helped him find an apartment with sparse furnishings, located between Wayne State University and the crime-infested Cass Corridor. Not yet a man, he was on his own while most kids don't emancipate from their families fully until age 24. Which road would Santino travel? Would the streets lure a wayward youth looking for excitement down Cass Corridor? Or, would the promise of the university environment help him to a life of security and productivity. Santino is currently completing a degree in chemistry and biochemistry. He credits a specific moment when he was alone and staring out of his independent living studio apartment. As he looked onto downtown Detroit, he simply decided to take advantage of the opportunities that were before him.

Doreatha also grew up in Detroit as a young woman of color. "My mom, at a young age, became a single mother and my father was a statistic dad. Not having much of anything, I started to 'get it' in a dangerous lifestyle." Doreatha wanted to turn her life around but had no real support system except for a frail grandmother. She was enrolled in the Bridges Towards Responsible Adulthood program. "They helped me learn how to become assertive, confident, and independent. It was a long and hard road to walk, but I thank the Lord for the wonderful staff who showed love to young women in need of help." Doreatha graduated from Henry Ford High School and received a scholarship to Lawrence Technological University. A recent challenge was the death of her grandmother. "I'm still working toward my goals and dreams to become the best woman I can be. My life will be dedicated to my grandma, Dessie Ree Kennerly."

Even with social support, it is unreasonable to expect that long-standing patterns totally disappear. Research shows that even youth who benefit from treatment programs usually have some continuing involvement in a prohibited activity such as alcohol consumption or minor delinquency. The vast majority of college freshman males have been reporting similar delinquent acts for 50 years. An all-or-nothing approach to measuring treatment success is fool hardy and unfair.

We tell young adults there will be speed bumps on the road to success. Rather than looking at backsliding as a total failure, these can be seen as temporary setbacks. A. P. Goldstein invokes concepts from relapse prevention where a lapse becomes a positive opportunity for further learning. Two-thirds of adults and teens treated for substance abuse will relapse at least once. Relapse can be viewed as the result of entrenched learning of old patterns rather than addictive disease. The youth is given skills to embrace a healthy lifestyle and friends who support positive change.[42]

Educator W. E. B. Du Bois once said, only responsibility teaches responsibility. Youth must become co-workers with adults in building their own destinies. However, only people who believe in the dignity and potential of young people will be comfortable treating them as partners in developing positive schools and communities. But we need not continue to be a society that fears, oppresses, and discards its most strong-willed young citizens.

Generosity: The Spirit of Helping

Help thy brother's boat across and lo! thine own has reached the shore.

—Hindu Proverb

Kurt Hahn, founder of Outward Bound, put the spirit of service at the center of his educational approach. He concluded that modern youth suffer from the "misery of unimportance" and long to be needed in some demanding cause. An "I'll-get-mine" culture leaves students self-absorbed and devoid of purpose.

When generosity is not in style, the task is to make caring fashionable and get young people "hooked on helping."

Service-Learning

I feel that the greatest thing one could give to another student is friendship. People who come from a negative home life, [school] is all they can look forward to and count on. I try to be nice to people and talk to people no one else will. I try to make them feel good about themselves. I do it a lot.

—Lance[43]

The service-learning movement is a revival of the spirit of generosity that is at the heart of all great ethical systems. The Christian, Jewish, Muslim, Hindu, and Buddhist faiths all extol the value of extending kindness to others, even strangers. Even in business and in industry the prevailing materialism is giving way to a new concern about providing opportunities for meeting the workers' needs for service.

High technology economies do not have the capacity of absorbing a mass of adolescents in formal employment roles. Yet there are limitless opportunities for volunteer service in addressing unmet needs in every community. Service is an antidote to narcissism and ill-being common in modern youth. Giving to others develops higher levels of moral development and provides teenagers with a sense of purpose.[44] Young people discover they have the power to influence their world in a positive manner.

Service-learning can teach prosocial values to youth with self-centered and antisocial lifestyles. An account of one school's experience with service-learning is *Nasty Girls, Thugs, and Humans Like Us*.[45] A high school faculty decided that all students would be given some volunteer job in their school. The coaches chose athletes as aides, while the bright kids worked in the office. Jobs were found for all except the students with lousy reputations. Someone suggested putting the "thugs" and kindred types in the special education rooms for severely developmentally disabled children. In that setting, the troublemakers caused no trouble at all but shined in service. They accompanied disabled students to the cafeteria and spread friendship that had never been forthcoming from the "good" students in the school.

Service-learning can infuse the curriculum.[46] A group of teens can wear "Special Olympics Staff" t-shirts. Young children could buy groceries for needy families using money accumulated as a result of no breakage or vandalism in their school. Teens with learning disabilities can serve as reading buddies to young children. Youth with sight could accompany students from a nearby school for the blind on camping trips. Other examples: Skits can be presented by students at a day care center; English students could study the essay "The Gift" and design a service activity; special education students could prepare a home and yard for a new refugee family, planting flowers and bringing toys to welcome the children.

Service-learning faces a challenge with self-centered and narcissistic youth. Initially, some buck the idea of giving their self to others. Needing to appear strong, they are vulnerable to criticism from peers if they show their gentler side. Successful service-learning programs makes caring trendy with youth who have been self-centered. Service begins in the circle of the school and then extends to the community.

Bobby Gilliam describes the use of service-learning with a group of students who had conspired to conceal information about a hidden firearm. In place of the typical consequence, such as time out, they were given a challenge responsibility. Their consequence was developing a project to make their campus safe. After initial resistance, they created very effective programs for drug awareness week. Through this experience, they gained positive status with other students and were bonded to the school staff.[47]

Service-learning knows no national boundaries. In Germany, the Catholic church developed programs for neo-Nazi youth. Young people guilty of hate crimes traveled with staff to Poland for six months of work to help build Holocaust memorials. They also gathered oral histories from elderly persons who lost their families in the Holocaust. The Protestant church takes troubled youth for similar trips to impoverished nations such as India to do volunteer work with homeless street children in health and recreation. Such programs are truly basic training or eye-opening for the conscience.

Once young people become hooked on helping, they often desire to continue service. This poses an ironic situation: Youth who previously were the societal liabilities are now potential assets. Schools and communities may have few appropriate roles for such adolescents. Father William Wasson of Friends of the Orphans solves this by making coworkers out of his students.

Father Wasson was the year 2000 winner of Kellogg's Hannah Neil World of Children award.[48] After 45 years, he is still active in the organization he founded, Nuestros Pequeños Hermanos or "Our Little Brothers and Sisters." Says Father Wasson, "It's surprising what you can do in a lifetime if you do it just a little at a time." In his case, this added up to a network of homes and schools that has provided families for 10,000 orphaned and abandoned children in six Latin American countries. Brothers and sisters are always kept together; in recent years, this includes many children orphaned by AIDS. The entire fabric of Friends of the Orphans is woven around the service ethic.

Children are taught to share and give back what was given to them. Younger students dedicate a "Year of Service" before starting high school. During this year they care for their younger brothers and sisters, work in the kitchen, office, farm, or some other role. After completing high school, they complete a second Year of Service, often traveling to NPH (Nuestros Pequeños Hermanos) homes in other countries. A typical day might find these "young staff" recruiting children who live in a local garbage dump, bringing them to school, bathing them, distributing clean clothes, feeding them, and welcoming them into the family. Some go on to complete a university education and return as permanent staff members.[49]

Engaging in service for its benefits would be just another variety of economic narcissism.[50] Genuine helping requires a spirit of generosity by reaching out in empathy to help another. The philosopher Martin Buber concludes: Those who set out to help others to satisfy their own needs are using others as objects. An authentic relationship is grounded in a deep respect for the other.[51]

The Oneness of Humankind

When we reach an acceptance of the differences that exist between people, then we begin to see them simply as human beings, not by their genders or skin color, race, or religion. We have created so many labels that we cannot see through them to the soul of the human being.

—Arun Gandhi[52]

Arun Gandhi lost his grandfather, Mahatma Gandhi (1869-1948) to an assassin. The elder Gandhi always taught his followers never to hate because such is the way of racism. Now, generations after the civil rights movement, we are still divided by our differences, and we fail to see the soul of our fellow human beings.

The late tennis great Arthur Ashe wrote that "being African American in America was more difficult for me to endure than having AIDS."[53] Most whites don't have a clue about what he meant; blacks know exactly how he felt. Jack Kirkland explains that persons of color seldom share their true feelings across the racial divide. Whites who have sanitized superficial relationships with polite, middle-class blacks are unaware of the depth of racial distrust. In this multicultural century, we must break down the barriers of race or suffer the consequences together.[54]

Jamie Chambers is an African American psychologist who grew up in Los Angeles and Denver. Although he runs a highly successful counseling practice for youth, he describes how years of exposure to racism in this culture leave him and many other people of color operating on the edge of vigilance. "As a victim of racism, I find myself leery of opening myself to a new relationship for fear it will permit another to 'pounce' on my already tattered spirit."[55]

Nathan Rutstein and Reginald Newkirk, who have developed Institutes for Healing Racism, say there is only one race, the human race. They use no polite words in calling racism a disease, much like mental illnesses, marked by distorted thinking and behavior.[56] Deep-seated mindsets of superiority and inferiority affect all people in our culture. Most whites who don't see themselves as racist are unaware of the privilege that comes to them from their illicit superior status.

The notion of "race" is itself rooted in ignorance. Sorting humans into categories was the brainchild of biologist Carolus Linnaeus (1707–1778), who ran out of plants and animals to classify. He then invented rankings for humans with "Caucasian" on the top.[57] Two centuries after Linnaeus passed away, racial healing has not been achieved. The cure to racism is in healing individual hearts and minds. This philosophy underlies Institutes for the Healing of Racism sponsored by schools and community organizations.

In most schools racial distrust, hurt, or superiority lies just below the surface. Several years ago, we became involved in training staff and community leaders at the Institutes for the Healing of Racism. This training is now being extended to students. Tom Tate, who directs our Ohio programs, studied student attitudes about race in a multi-ethnic alternative school.[58] After considerable multicultural education, subtle racism was still abundant. White students surveyed believed that issues surrounding racism were openly and productively discussed while significant numbers of black students disagreed. Tate found that many black students carefully observed how school staff treated one another and perceived patterns of racism invisible to white students. In general, most white students believed "We all get along here." Black students had many unspoken concerns and were open to discussing racism in their school. Most white students were uncomfortable in opening up such topics.

While subtle prejudice remains buried, schools cannot escape dealing with strong hatred by groups of students who build an identity by violent opposition to people who differ in race, religion, and/or sexual orientation. In some respects, blatant hostility is easier to confront since it is not masked. Tom Tate provides this example:

> Jason was a white supremacist skinhead. He put swastikas on his notebook, wore the confederate flag, and promoted the KKK. He recruited two other white youths as lieutenants in his campaign to stir hatred of black students. Equally racist was Raul, a black youth. His father was killed in a white bar where he had stopped to ask for directions. Raul hated whites and wasn't shy about letting them know it. The challenge to staff was helping these hate-filled students see one another as human beings. In time, each became a solid member of a positive, integrated group. After Jason graduated, a new white youth was enrolled who was just as bigoted. How would Raul handle this? He astounded

staff by inviting this new student to be his roommate and they became close friends.

The Institutes for the Healing of Racism is committed to the principle of the oneness of humankind. A typical group includes two or three dozen diverse participants led by co-facilitators of different racial backgrounds. Formal presentations on the history and pathology of racism stimulate personal reflection and dialogue in a safe environment. As students become comfortable sharing viewpoints seldom voiced outside of one's racial group, empathy develops. Through this transformation, true friendships are forged. People who were once distrustful because of skin color, come to like—maybe even to love—one another, rather than just tolerate each other.[59]

The place to begin healing racism in institutes is with the staff. All personnel in our school, from bus drivers to the board of trustees, participated in Institutes for the Healing of Racism.[60] Describing his experience, Martin Mitchell wrote: "I have come to the realization that abuse of power, acts of superiority, and dehumanization are among the greatest threats we face as humanity. The devastating disease of racism separates us as human beings and the only cure is to heal as one family. Having experienced the healing process, I have great hope for the future despite the many dehumanizing events that are etched in my consciousness every day."[61]

Conclusion

At the core of positive youth development are opportunities for belonging, mastery, independence, and generosity. The powerful need for belonging is met through positive relationships with adults and peers. Effective programs also require teamwork among significant adults who provide children with support and limits. Students develop mastery in schools that kindle the desire for learning and teach youth to resolve conflicts in a respectful manner. Independence can only be developed through opportunities in exercising personal responsibility and planning one's future. Finally, generosity is the core civic virtue that allows people of diverse backgrounds to live in harmony. It takes a concerted effort of a community to meet the needs of young people. In the final chapter, we provide a seven-step roadmap for building courage in all children and helping our most challenging youth to reclaim themselves.

Works Cited

[1] Chambers. 2001.

[2] Hall. 1829.

[3] Fahlberg. 1991.

[4] Garmezy. 1994.

[5] Perlman. 1979.

[6] Brown. 1983. Seita and Brendtro. 2001.

[7] Safran and Muran. 2000.

[8] Trieschman, Whittaker, and Brendtro. 1967.

[9] Brendtro and Ness. 1983.

[10] Brendtro. 1998.

[11] Harris. 1998.

[12] St. Augustine describes his youthful indiscretions in his *Confessions*. St. Francis was called "Frenchy the Chief" by fellow members of his gang, "The Gay Brigade," according to columnist L. M. Boyd. 1999.

[13] Garner. 1982.

[14] Brendtro and Mitchell. 1983. Larry Brendtro and Joan Bacon. 1995. Mitchell and Ameen. 1985. Martin Mitchell. 1982.

[15] Gold and Osgood. 1992.

[16] Steinberg. 1994.

[17] Dryfoos. 1994.

[18] Montessori. 1967, 1995.

[19] Odney and Brendtro. 1992.

[20] Lantieri. 2001.

[21] Lantieri and Patti. 1996.

[22] Mendler and Curwin. 1999.

[23] Garrity, Jens, Porter, Sager, and Short-Camilli. 2000.

[24] Hawkins. 1994.

[25] Walker and Severson. 1992.

[26] Rhode, Jensen, and Reavis. 1996.

[27] For a compendium of interventions grounded in behavioral research see Walker, Colvin, and Ramsey. 1995. Psychoeducational interventions draw from ecological, cognitive, behavioral, and developmental research as described by Wood, Brendtro, Fecser, and Nichols. 1999.

[28] Sprick, Garrison, and Howard. 1998. The Safe and Civil Schools program includes a range of publications, videotapes, and training opportunities. For information, contact Sopris West, P.O. Box 1809, Longmont, CO 80502-1809. www.sopriswest.com.

[29] Long, Fecser, and Wood. 2001.

[30] The psychoeducational foundations of LSCI are described by Long, Fecser, and Wood. 2001. For information on the Safe and Reclaiming Schools program or Life Space Crisis Intervention training contact Starr Commonwealth, Albion, MI 49224. www.starr.org.

[31] Knitzer, Steinberg, and Fleisch, 1990.

[32] McCall. 1996.

[33] Gold and Osgood. 1992.

[34] Benedict. 1938.

[35] Liepmann. 1928.

[36] Varenhorst. 1984.

[37] Wasmund and Tate. 1995.

[38] Brendtro and Bacon. 1992.

[39] Gabor and Greene. 1991.

[40] Anglin. 1992.

[41] Harkins. 1991.

[42] Goldstein and Martens. 2000.

[43] Odney and Brendtro. 1992.

[44] Larson and Brendtro. 2000.

[45] Murray-Seegert. 1989.

[46] Brendtro. 1986.

[47] Gilliam, Nicholas, and Saap. 2000.

[48] The Kellogg's Hannah Neil World of Children Award is named for humanitarians W. K. Kellogg, who gave his entire fortune to establish the Kellogg Foundation, and Hannah Neil, who founded one of the nation's early children's charities in Columbus, Ohio. The honorary chairperson for the award is Muhammad Ali. Information on this award is available at www.starr.org

[49] Friends of the Orphans. 2000.

[50] Saurman and Nash. 1980.

[51] Buber. 1970.

[52] B'Hahn. 2001.

[53] Ashe and Rampersad. 1993.

[54] Kirkland. 2000.

[55] Chambers. 2000.

[56] Newkirk and Rutstein. 2000.

[57] Kivel. 1996.

[58] From unpublished studies by Thomas Tate, Starr Commonwealth, Van Wert, OH.

[59] Rutstein. 2000.

[60] The Kellogg Company, The Kellogg Foundation, and State Farm Insurance have contributed to set up this training institute. Because of Starr's success in operating Institutes for the Healing of Racism, this idea has spread to other community and corporate organizations, and a national center for the healing of racism was begun. Each year, conferences are held in various locations to train educators and youth workers to be more effective with children of color. For information phone 517-629-5593 or see the Web site www.starr.org.

[61] Martin Mitchell cited by Newkirk and Rutstein. 2000.

chapter five

Promising Futures

My grandmother, the one who raised me, said to me, "If you walk up a path that somebody else told you to walk, and you look ahead and you don't like where you're going, and you look back and you don't want to return, step off the path. Pick yourself a brand new road."

—Maya Angelou[1]

Tony's life path had been littered with damaged relationships. Now he was immersed in a network of human bonds that would point his life in a new direction. This boy, who had never gotten

along with peers, was learning to live and work with a diverse group of peers. In the residences, the mature women who served as surrogate mothers were particularly important to most boys living away from home. These women provided a stability that many youth had not known from their own mothers. Few had advanced training but they brought rich experiences and deep commitment to the youth. Best of all, they were huggable. College-age students who served as recreation staff helped to provide positive role models and a more high-powered version of youth care.

Heading the counseling staff was Al Lily, a former teacher who went on to earn a graduate degree in social work. Floyd Starr was leery of therapists who thought kids could be changed by "the 50-minute hour." But he trusted Al Lily who shared his philosophy of environmental therapy and loved kids. Lily explained, "Many students entered with very little self-control. When at first adults had to exercise external control, they talked to the student about self-control. Students started out in highly structured cottages. When they learned to be responsible, they earned their way to more relaxed, ranch-style residences. By making good decisions, they were preparing to return to the community. They also gained insight into how their own families had broken down, and they learned a new style of family living." Lily saw the big picture: He was training troubled youth for their future role as positive parents. Said Lily, "The cycle of abuse has to be broken."

Mr. Lily chose Jerry to be Tony's counselor. Jerry was a zestful young man who in later years became a decorated sea captain. He was a pied piper for hard-to-reach kids. Tony had been caged like an animal for three months and was very guarded. Jerry had little to go on, as the case files had been "sanitized." The expert on Tony would have to be Tony himself, who had never trusted adults.

Youth who fear rejection and feel shame long for love and want to share their hurt. Yet they still believe that if an admired adult were to discover their secrets, they would be rejected again. Experience taught Jerry that Tony needed time to find the

*courage to trust. Counselors didn't need to probe into the past,
for in their own time, students usually opened up of their own
volition. Every child has a story to tell if an adult can be found
who is worthy of trust. Tony found that person in Jerry.*

*Counselors consulted with one another on difficult problems.
Jerry was still in his twenties and realized he was more of a big
brother than a father figure or therapist. He believed that Tony
would benefit from a more mature and seasoned counselor. So
Jerry and Mr. Lily decided to invite Max to join Tony's treatment
team. Max was a former Ohio State Police officer who was also
much admired by the students. Six-foot-four and middle-aged,
Max, was a gentle fatherly role model. Now Tony had two strong
male role models who believed in him.*

*In retrospect, what Tony needed most was probably not psychi-
atric treatment but stable adults who provided him with support
and guidance. Fire setting was but a symptom of many unmet
needs in Tony's life. Jerry and Max decided to focus on present
and future challenges. Tony needed to learn to bond to adults,
respect authority, get along with peers, be a friend, succeed in
school, plan for a vocation, and find a purpose in life. In today's
terms, these were strength-based interventions. "Our goal," said
Jerry, "was to immerse students in experiences that helped them
make sense out of their lives. We tried to provide as many normal growth opportunities as possible. As they surmounted challenges, they built confidence in themselves."*

*Many traumatized youth don't want to keep dredging up a
painful past that cannot be changed. But if guilt and shame fes-
ter, self-destructive behavior follows. Problems of guilt were
often handled with spiritual counseling, which was Father
Pellett's realm. Every Sunday Father Pellett led boys in the rite
of confession, proclaiming that every sin, however great, could
be forgiven. For those who wondered if this covered their
"whoppers," the chaplain's office was available for private confession. In this little congregation of worldly wise boys, sinners
sometimes had to stand in line. At Our Lady of Angels school,
Tony savored any attention he received from the two priests.
Here was another kindly man he could call father.*

School wasn't anything like Tony had known. Classes were small and most teachers took an interest in him just like Sister Carolan once had. In this bounty of role models, Principal Kent Esbaugh was yet another father figure. He was not the least intimidated by kids who hated school. He had left a career as a principal and coach in public schools in order to work with these highly challenging students. Kent was impressed that there were many like Tony who were intelligent but who had had lousy experiences in school. He knew that in order to succeed with them, it was important to treat these young people with honesty and respect. Even if he had to be tough, his students knew they could always come and talk about their problems.

While Esbaugh had strong expectations for academic success, he believed creative and expressive curricula were equally important. Automotive and wood shop as well as creative arts were popular. Just as in the cottages, the boys helped keep their school and classrooms immaculate. Students who once vandalized schools took pride in this place. While the teachers at the time were not trained in special education, they gave abundant individualized attention. Espaugh said, "We always had students with very serious problems. Once they get their lives organized, they can turn around and be very positive." Esbaugh saw school success as a powerful therapy. Routines of responsibility stabilized disorganized lives. Students would enter with miserable school records and leave with a rekindled interest in learning.

For more than three years Tony was re-parented and re-educated: An alienated boy learned to belong; a failing student found success; an out of control adolescent learned responsibility; and a self-absorbed youth became a friend to others. Grade eleven was the upper limit of the school's curriculum at the time. Most students returned home to finish high school. But this was the era of Viet Nam and youth turning 17 could go directly into the armed services. Military recruiters were hunting for young men who would respect authority, work as a team member, and get along with diverse groups of people. Tony qualified on all counts. He decided on his future and, with the court's approval, he enlisted in the marines.

Tony's time in Michigan came to a close. From being a boy who was a risk to the community, he was now a strong young man set out to risk his own life in the service of his country. Tony was among the last of over 10,000 students to pass through Starr during the tenure of its founder. While Tony was serving in Viet Nam, Floyd Starr retired at 84 years of age.

After completing his tour of duty, Tony returned to civilian life. His goal was to build a future totally unlinked to his troubled past. In later years, investigative journalists would uncover pieces of his story; however, they rigorously protected his privacy. When interviewed in his mid-forties by author John Kuenster, Tony was reluctant to look back. "I don't want to open old wounds. I might say something wrong. I want to forget it."[2]

Tony was able to quietly take his place among millions of other citizens in the state where he chose to make his home. Today, he is not a hero who is changing the world. He is a quiet citizen doing his part. He wants little more than to live his life in privacy. We honor these wishes and end his story here.

Our Lady of Angels has also left its past behind. Today the building once gutted by fire stands again as a center of hope and learning for the African American and Latino students now enrolled there. Although the Our Lady of Angels fire records have never been officially closed, most who have researched this story conclude that this was likely the worst loss of life from arson in American history.

A close friend of Judge Alfred J. Cilella recalls the incredible stress that accompanied the hearings on this case. "He took a real beating from all corners, and it had a very detrimental effect. It wasn't long after that he got sick and died."[3] Had he lived to see the fruits of his decision, the judge would have had the satisfaction of knowing that he had been faithful to the code of the children's court: "To serve the moral, emotional, mental, and physical welfare of the minor and the best interests of the community."

Some might say that a child guilty of serious crimes doesn't deserve a second chance, that society would be better served by caging such a kid for life. For half a century, Floyd Starr encountered that criticism. To those quick to condemn, he would recite a passage he knew by heart: "My brothers, if someone is caught in a sin, you who are spiritual should restore him with a spirit of gentleness. But watch yourself, lest you also be tempted." These were the words of a mass murderer turned theologian, St. Paul, writing to the Galatians.

In these times, many rail at evil and call for retribution. But vengeance never leads to restoration or spiritual healing. Few have exemplified the spirit of forgiveness as powerfully as Martin Luther King, Jr. Of those who wished him malice, he said, "When we look beneath the surface, beneath the impulsive evil deed, we see within our enemy-neighbor a measure of goodness and know that the viciousness and evilness of his acts are not quite representative of all that he is. We see him in a new light."[4]

A Better Way

Why shouldn't we go out then and give the murderer what he deserves?
And yet there is a better way.
The murderer who has hurt us shall become a relative.

—Ella Deloria[5]

Wherever humans live in community, two competing solutions for preserving social order have arisen: retribution and restoration. Retribution seeks to hurt or banish the offender. Restoration aims to heal and restore harmony to the community.[6] Tribal cultures, such as the First Nations peoples of North America and the Maori of New Zealand, have long employed restorative justice to return rule-breakers to the social bond. Restoration is the preferred goal in Muslim and Pacific Rim societies. It is also a central theme in Biblical stories of redemption.[7]

Prior to the Norman Conquest, most villages in Europe solved conflicts by requiring the offender to make amends with the victim. But William the Conqueror decreed that crime was a disruption of the "king's peace." He established courts to collect fines, payment that once went to victims. The king became wealthy. The dominant method of justice shifted from restoration to retribution.

Seven Habits for Courageous Communities

What we want to achieve in our work with young people is to find and strengthen the positive and healthy elements, no matter how deeply they are hidden. We enthusiastically believe in the existence of those elements even in the seemingly worst of our adolescents.

—Karl Wilker, 1921[8]

From the world over are calls for a rebirth of restoration in our schools and communities. The theme of the Children's Defense Fund and a Republican presidential campaign was "Leave no child behind." The presiding judge of what was the world's first juvenile court declares "We cannot afford to fail them."[9] A society that values its young will treat all children as our children.[10] A community that fails to care for the least advantaged makes all young people vulnerable.

It will take concerted effort if we are to leave no child behind. This requires building courage in all children and restoring those who are discouraged. We need a fresh mind-set, a vision of potentials where once only problems were visible. A wealth of research-validated methods are available to cultivate competence in children. We also need to develop organizational capacity and rebuild the youth development infrastructure of our communities.[11] In this final section, we borrow the "seven-habits" metaphor from Stephen Covey to describe these critical transformations.

1. Creating a Vision

The first step on the pathway to changing individuals or systems is to set a vision. Powerful restorative environments are marked by a unifying theme, a set of beliefs shared by members of that organizational community. The vision statement provides a way of building, belonging, and setting priorities. Students, teachers, parents, board members, and others participate in developing the vision statement. This document can be prominently displayed and frequently discussed. Applicants for positions in schools can be screened to ascertain whether they hold beliefs that are compatible with the school's core values. The organization sets goals to implement its vision. Each organization must create its own statement of core values. To illustrate, this is the vision statement developed by a community youth collaboration.[12]

A Vision Statement for Children and Families

➜ **Children are rich resources who can benefit our communities.**

Children can be enlisted to be creative, active, caring, and involved. They can be perceived as part of the solution, rather than a problem. Encouraging youth as partners can begin at a very early age and will have the effect of creating more socially aware, self-confident, and capable young people. Rather than always imposing things on children, we must elicit their ideas, their solutions, and their creative energies. Children are capable of helping themselves and others if adults are there to guide and support them in these endeavors.

➜ Young people are our social equals.

Treating young people as social equals means that our behaviors and attitudes flow from an assumption that adults are not better than children. This does not imply an absence of guidelines and rules, but demands that we examine our practices to ensure that adults don't demean young people or their abilities. Too often, children are treated as second-class citizens. We hold different and higher expectations for young people than we do for adults. As social equals, youths are entitled to respect and responsibility.

➜ Children can develop problem-solving skills, prosocial character traits, and healthy self-concepts.

We must possess and act upon a fundamental belief that people, including children, can change. This change can go beyond the surface behaviors to meaningful, lasting changes in character traits that drive behavior. We cannot give up on children, even when the situation seems hopeless. If we focus our energies on the capacities rather than the deficiencies present in the child, transformation is possible.

➜ Children's physical, educational, social, spiritual, and emotional needs must be met.

Even though society appears to have accepted this as a guiding principle, we often don't act upon it. An aura of helplessness seems to surround the plight of children. We believe that all children have a right to have all of their physical and intangible needs met. Unimaginable waste of human potential is accepted whenever we assume, for example, that it's appropriate to have a ten percent drop-out rate in our schools or that over 20 percent of children live in poverty.

➜ Families are the best environments for healthy development of children, but everyone can help.

We all want to see children nurtured and cared for in a secure home environment. Even when this is the case, we have a responsibility to ensure that children are successful. A teacher, mentor, or adult friend can provide a bond and connection that helps a child see his or her potential. Where a family cannot provide for all of the child's needs, other adults must rise to the challenge to help. A caring person who can look beyond a young person's outward behavior to see his or her inner struggle can make the difference between disappointment and achievement.

➜ Every child succeeds; no child fails.

It's simple—our goal is that everyone makes it. We cannot look around a classroom or playground to choose who will thrive and who will not. Any child who does not reach his or her full potential is a loss that we will not accept. We want all of our children to be educated, nurtured, and physically, spiritually, and emotionally healthy.

2. Nurturing our Families

Parenting patterns learned in childhood are often replicated in the next generation. Those who grow up with positive experiences build strong character and self-worth and become positive parents. Children raised amidst abuse and neglect often perpetuate these same patterns with their own children.[13]

We must help all parents nurture their children if we are to break the cycle of careless parenting.[14] Research shows four patterns of abusive and negligent parenting. These patterns are (1) inappropriate expectations, (2) lack of empathy toward children's needs, (3) parental belief in physical punishment, and (4) parental role reversal. Parent education can address each of these pitfalls. Parents can learn to have expectations appropriate to their child's developmental level. They gain empathy as they discover how to read the feelings of their children. The logic behind physical punishment is examined; however, many parents don't want to give in and still desire to show them who's boss. They will need new methods of discipline in place of physical violence. Finally, parents who are helpless and reverse roles by expecting their children to care for them are given the confidence to provide their children love and limits.

A rich array of family support programs provides education, family therapy, and intensive in-home intervention. Another strategy is to recreate the sense of tribe or extended family in our communities. Margaret Harrison founded HOME-START in England as a way of providing support to high risk young mothers, many in their teens. The plan is simple and powerful. Mature women are matched to young mothers and serve in a role similar to one provided in stable, multi-generation extended families. These matches may endure for years, and the children look at the HOME-START volunteers as family members. This program has been operating long enough that some children who grew up in HOME-START families are now becoming adult volunteers themselves.[15]

"Families have screwed up these kids for 15 years; how are we supposed to fix them?" Such negative attitudes are widespread. Schools need to reach out and engage families, but our language betrays our biases. Parents of youth with problems are seen as inadequate, confused, and unmotivated. A favorite professional term for bashing parents is dysfunctional. Barbara Huff of the Federation of Families for Children's Mental Health calls this a blaming and condescending term. Any parent of a child with problems has encountered dysfunctional professionals. She suggests that we reserve this disrespectful adjective for describing dysfunctional systems.

Even those most committed to troubled children seldom exert much effort to help the child's parents. Perhaps we believe that parents are not workable. This is a self-fulfilling prophecy where we write off the family without really trying. Some programs seem designed to keep parents at bay; practices that weaken the bond between child and family constitute malpractice. We must work to maintain a close bond between a youth and his or her family—it is among the most important predictors of success.

Schools need to be parent-friendly so teachers do not feel intimidated by parents. Although recognizing the value of parent participation, teachers have little training in working with parents. Parents often feel alienated from professionals and intimidated by strange jargon. Schools can be impersonal bureaucracies that are hard to influence. Parents may sense they are blamed for the problems of their children. Too often, a mutual blame game results; parents believe that problems are caused by schools while educators are equally convinced that parents are the problem.[16] When parents form advocacy groups, this can enhance collaboration or intensify adversarial encounters.

A family-friendly philosophy respects and empowers parents. Families are involved in volunteer roles, parent support groups, and parent advisory boards. Families also receive skills to support their children. The PACER Center in Minneapolis helps families of youth with disabilities. Parents from around the country have been trained as advocates in the justice system for the rights of children with disabilities.[17] Advocacy groups like The Federation of Families for Children's Mental Health and Children and Adults with Attention Deficit Disorders [CHADD] have affiliates nationwide to be the voice of parents. Each has publications to keep parents abreast of issues and advances with challenging children and youth.[18]

Every organization needs to solicit feedback from the parents themselves in order to include them in teamwork relationships. As one parent said, "I know I have limits as a mother. But I have been watching and worrying over my child for 15 years. Do they think I know nothing?"

3. Connecting to Our Students

According to Richard Foster, the dean of American educational consultants, the biggest task facing schools in the twenty-first century will be to reverse the process of depersonalization that began over a century ago when schools adopted a factory model.[19] We asked Dr. Foster to share his vision on transforming schools into family-like learning communities. This is what he told us:[20]

> Today many spend more time communicating via e-mail or voice mail than through direct personal contact. In such a technological society, we must guard against losing the bonds of human relationship. A lot of children say, "I have a couple of good teachers." When asked what makes those teachers good, the students usually say, "They care about me." Students are very alert to the messages adults convey. Street youth in particular are vigilant and pick up quickly on our nonverbal behaviors. They can tell if we care or not.

At Burbank Junior High School in Los Angeles, we had a ninth-grade girl who looked like she belonged anywhere but at school. She had been absent the day before, and one teacher greeted her, "Mary, where were you? I missed you. We really want you here!" Mary behaved perfectly the entire period. In her next class, the teacher said, "Oh, I see you've decided to come to school today." Mary raised hell for that whole period.

We build big schools to save money but this is a false economy because it destroys community. Schools must reverse a century of depersonalization. Large schools can be broken apart until each has a maximum of 750 students in high school, 400 students in middle school, and 350 students in elementary school. Ideally, schools can be further subdivided into small classrooms that operate like families.

Once we view a school as an extended family, we change how we treat one another. We don't kick out of our family children with problems, so we shouldn't even begin to use the threat of suspension. Instead, we intensify open communication and problem solving. In times of crisis, we conduct conferences with a student and his or her parents. The goal is to move all members of our school family toward success and leave no one behind. A great myth is that the solution to school problems will be found in policy manuals full of rules. There are only two rules that are really important: You can't hurt yourself and you can't hurt others.

An educator said, "We have had 500 suspensions so far this year." What purpose does this serve? A lot of these juveniles know how to pull the chains of adults in order to get time off, especially during hunting season. Expulsion from schools is hopefully a practice of the past where only the powerful have rights. We are saying in a sense, "You don't have the right to learn. It is a privilege we adults control."

Violence is not the right word to describe what is wrong with schools. A closed system that leaves some children out is already a violent place. The problem comes when we allow the creation of in-groups and out-groups. It is hell to be left out if you are 16. If you fail or are ostracized, there are only a few things you can do. Many students abandon school, while others fight back. Most problems of school violence result from closed systems. We need to ask ourselves these questions: Do persons of all racial, socioeconomic, or religious backgrounds fit in? Do students who act differently or those who wear "strange" clothes belong? If not, the students are likely to do strange things. These problems won't be stopped by more guards and metal detectors, but by including all children. Athletic teams, drama troupes, and other school group activities can create positive gangs. Every child needs to join one.

"Adults don't talk to us," many students say. We need to engage *every* child, even if it is with some simple question like, "How is it going?" Adults also need to watch the nonverbal signals and be able to spot a child in pain so we can reach out and touch these children. "I hope you will come back tomorrow" must be clearly communicated in word and action. Many of our students come from very challenging backgrounds, and these students in particular need to know we support them. Some are ashamed of their parents, as if their parents' limitations are their faults also. We can tell them that they are not responsible for what others do; they can only be responsible for what they do.

Students don't need teachers who interfere with their learning. It is estimated that 15 percent of teachers are peak performers;

they are very creative but often don't get reports in on time because they like working with children and think paperwork is not worth their time. The next 75 percent can become very effective as they develop their skills over a period of three to five years. Finally, we have the ten percent who are "walking protoplasm." They are already dead but nobody knows how to bury them. Our job is to protect our children from them. These teachers must change or leave, because they are abusive and try to discard students they don't want to teach.

Schools are by nature conservative organizations and will not change radically. To create effective reform, we must concentrate on a few specific goals. Each year we ask schools to select two or three goals and then specify strategies to help them reach the desired results. These goals become the performance contracts against which we can measure how schools are doing. A list of goals for schools to get back to basics in the twenty-first century would be:

1. Every child has one significant adult in school who cares about him or her.

2. Every child is seen as a learner, treated as a learner, succeeds as a learner.

3. Every child develops skills to resolve conflict and communicate respectfully.

A candidate for school superintendent was asked what he would do about students at risk. His answer was simple yet profound, and he was selected to lead that school: "All of our kids are at risk. Some of our students have good coping skills. We need to teach those same skills to those who don't have them."

4. Connecting Youth to Positive Peers

We began piloting programs to build positive peer cultures 30 years ago. Instead of focusing on the negative aspects of peer groups, we enlisted the group as a positive force in peer-helping, thereby giving students the opportunity to care. We have high expectations for positive behavior; caring is the core value.

Anything or anyone that hurts themself or others will be challenged. This is perhaps the most consistent "zero-tolerance" model.

There are two main ways adults can help provide positive peer influence. These involve *protecting* youth from negative peers and the process of *transforming* negative groups. Both strategies have research support, although each strategy approaches the problem with different assumptions.

Protecting youth from negative peers is a goal of every parent. This is particularly critical in high-risk neighborhoods. Successful urban families closely monitor their childrens' friendships and maximize time at home in order to protect them from negative influences.[21] Involvement with prosocial peers is a fundamental asset in positive youth development.

Since concentrated groups of antisocial youth tend to foster delinquent values, it makes sense to prevent these associations whenever possible. Multisystemic Treatment (MST) is a community-based program that attempts to keep troubled youth from any contact with similar peers. The program's recommendation is that such students not be placed together in special classrooms, treatment groups, and community activities so that delinquency is not fostered.[22] MST forcibly takes away youth from friends who don't meet adult approval. This involves implementing "very unpleasant consequences when the youth contacts antisocial peers—and positive consequences when the youth contacts positive peers."[23] Since most youth are loyal to their peers, breaking up friendships is not an easy thing to do. MST staff acknowledge that given the power of peer relationships, it is important to "prepare the parents for battle."

MST researchers believe that it is futile to try to change negative groups: "It seems unreasonable to expect that a group of youth with behavioral problems will somehow generate prosocial values and group norms by interacting with one another."[24] Other researchers go so far as to claim that any peer group treatment program with troubled youth is "iatrogenic," meaning it will make participants worse.[25] Pessimistic views can override the data.

In the best of worlds, all youths would hang out with positive peers. In reality, with such large numbers in schools and programs, they are in contact with many high risk and troubled youths. Entrenched negative peer cultures are like sourdough and keep regenerating. Through a not-so-simple process, negative group cultures can be changed. Positive youth cultures cannot be imposed by command or force, but by enlisting youths as resources instead of enemies. Such programs teach youth skills for peer helping and conflict resolution. Resolving Conflict Creatively Program (RCCP) was tailored to transform hostile urban school climates. Positive Peer Culture (PPC) has successfully reversed negative subcultures among youth at risk in alternative settings. The EQUIP peer-helping program teaches responsibility and fosters conscience development with antisocial students. All teachers consider students as potentially positive leaders and use them as partners in problem solving.

Abusus non tollit usus is a Latin phrase indicating that just because a method is abused, does not mean it is useless. In fact, there is abundant evidence that negative peer cultures can be converted into peer-helping. Two recent studies address that question. Martin Gold and D.W. Osgood tracked over 40 groups of students sent by courts to four different Michigan peer treatment programs. In groups with close ties to staff, antisocial values and behavior declined. When youth were reconnected to school, positive outcomes were more likely. The most effective teachers in these programs were able to simultaneously nurture needs and demand responsibility from students. They treated students with respect and were treated with respect in return. Both students with delinquent values and those who were emotionally troubled could benefit from peer-helping programs, although the troubled youth needed extra adult nurturance. Students in these settings felt secure and were not victimized. Six months after their release 80 percent were living in a community setting, and most were with family members.[26]

The EQUIP Program augments PPC with training of group members in anger management, moral development, and social skills.[27] Youth in the EQUIP program in an Ohio youth correctional facility had better school attendance and significantly less misconduct. At the one year follow-up, those with the tendency to relapse into previous behavior in the EQUIP program was 15 percent, whereas two control groups had 35 and 40 percent recidivism. These results suggest that peer-helping can have enduring positive impact on very difficult youth.

Most troubled youth want positive peers but don't know how to befriend them. Often they feel awkward around "good" kids who may subtly communicate rejection. Scott, a student, told us there was no way he could escape negative peers because he lives in the same house with his brother who carries weapons and deals in drugs. "I want to change but I think I won't live long if I do," he opined. He also felt obligated to support his mother. "My dad is in prison and won't let me visit because he thinks I turned him in for drug dealing." To make a clean break, Scott will virtually have to disown his family. If he does, who will be his new family? Who will reach out in friendship?

5. Healing Broken Spirits

A suicide note left by a teen read, "Not having a good enough reason to live is a good enough reason to die." This is a spiritual cry but many adults don't know how to respond. Young people who are spiritually empty may fail to develop a strong conscience or sense of purpose. Linda Lantieri has provided educators with a rich collection of ideas about how to develop what she calls "schools of spirit."[28] In such a school, conflict is transformed into healing. The goal is to build a community of values built on deep respect for one another.

The separation of church and state is a cherished principle in U.S. history. Nevertheless, many believe that a holistic approach to positive youth development must address the spiritual needs of students.[29] The traditional barriers between secular and sacred institutions are being reconsidered. Research on the protective factor of faith-based connections brings this topic into the mainstream of youth development. Communities of faith provide services and relationships not available in secular organizations. A New York youth center allows young people to experience the concept of a loving God to gain spiritual and moral capacity to lead productive lives. Scott Larson of Straight Ahead Ministries uses volunteers to mentor incarcerated and at-risk youth.[30]

Girls and Boys Town programs integrate relationships, skills, empowerment, and the spiritual quest.[31] The goal is not to convert youth but to offer opportunities for spiritual growth in several specific areas. Many youth have had negative experiences with religion and need to be exposed to the concept of a loving God. They are encouraged to participate in a faith community of their choosing. They learn the basic principles of that faith, and connect with pastors and other members of the faith community. Faith turns into action as they become role models along with their peers and incorporate their beliefs into their lifestyle. Val Peter sees two potential abuses of spiritual programs: intrusive devotion and the neglect of religion. Staff must ensure that there is a balance between extremes of these abuses.

Students at Starr Commonwealth have opportunities to participate in a full range of spiritual counseling, study groups, and creative activities with a spiritual theme. The "ministry arts" program integrates music, art, and the spiritual quest.[32] In formal classes students explore how youth can deal with issues of faith. The format follows artistic metaphors: the artist within, the search for meaning, drawing lines, taking a stand for positive change, the harmony of parts, finding inner peace, the critic's eye, learning from criticism, and celebrating joy. The visual or musical productions of these groups are used to enrich the community. It is moving when graduating students give farewell remarks at their last chapel service. They thank family, staff, and the peers who helped them transform their lives. They are powerful models for peers who may not yet have found hope and purpose.

Discussions relating to the issue of faith create dissonance for some, particularly those working in secular organizations. Then there are young people who are hungry to talk about spiritual issues. One youth put it this way: "I gave up trying to talk to adults about my spiritual concerns because when I brought it up, they got nervous and changed the subject." Adults should not be expected to provide spiritual guidance to youth if they are not so inclined or qualified. But we can help connect youth with people who can walk with them in their spiritual journey.

The Gan Wha School

A colleague from Taiwan told us of a time when that island still had cultural traditions of human sacrifice.[33] The natives believed that they must behead young maidens to prevent famine and pestilence. In the mid-nineteenth century, the island was ruled by the Manchu Dynasty. China sent governors to the aboriginal tribes. The most popular governor was Wu Fung who lived with these people for 30 years. They learned to trust him and eventually he was able to persuade them to stop human sacrifices. But then came disaster and floods. The tribal leaders came to Wu Fung and said, "The people are ready to revolt. We must have human sacrifice again. Only this will quiet them." Wu Fung, knowing that something drastic was needed, agreed. "Yes, this one time, but only once."

Wu Fung gave directions: On a certain night, all the people should gather at a particular banyan tree. A rider would come on a white horse wearing a red robe and a red hood. They should sacrifice this person without hesitation. So, the jubilant people gathered at the banyan tree. Excitement rose as the horse with the hooded rider approached at the appointed time. The rider was seized and beheaded. In the midst of the tumult, someone pulled back the hood and discovered that it was their friend and ruler, Wu Fung, whom they had killed. The people were so moved that he would give his life in place of one of them that they never again sacrificed humans.

The Chinese language has a word that cannot be translated into any other. The word is *Gan Wha*. It describes this change in the people as they replaced the darkness of fear and distrust with enlightened respect for all fellow humans. Today on the island of Taiwan there is a special school for students who are troubled, angry, and distrustful. It is named *Gan Wha School*, a place where the heart is changed.

6. Creating Programs of Integrity

Training and treatment approaches that aspire to help people lead more effective and satisfying lives must not be permitted to endure simply on the basis of the faith and enthusiasm of their proponents. All educational and treatment interventions should be subject to careful and continuing evaluation.[34]

The overarching goal of every school and youth program is to create lasting, positive development and change in young people. Many interventions have favorable short-term effects but these cannot be maintained over time. Arnold Goldstein and B. K. Martens suggest we no longer can afford to follow a "treat and hope" philosophy.[35] We may succeed at getting young people to jump through hoops, spit back trivial facts, jump to adult commands and say "Yes sir." These are not sufficient skills to operate independently and make sound life decisions.

Any enterprise needs quality control systems. Pilots follow checklists and have inspectors join them in the cockpit during flight. In our field, many are not even sure which indicators we should be watching in our educational cockpits. Outside rules for achievement testing tell little about the quality of the human learning environment. Because human relationships are the linchpin of effective intervention, we seek to measure the quality of the interpersonal environment. We need to know whether students trust peers and staff or whether interactions are based on coercion and intimidation. Does the staff feel part of a cohesive team and do they see themselves as adversaries of administration? How do students and families evaluate the services they receive?[36]

The *Audit of Educational Environments* is used to assess the factors critical to program quality.[37] This includes the physical environment, safety policies, and the order and structure of a school. In the interpersonal domain we test cultural competence, family/community partnerships, and youth empowerment. Does the school cultivate strengths and social responsibility in students? What is the style of leadership and teamwork? Perhaps the most critical element in the Audit is the statement of core values. This explicit set of beliefs about our mission becomes the basis for setting and evaluating our educational goals.

Father Val Peter of Girls and Boys Town says that any technology of education is worthless if we don't treat children with love and respect. He translates the dignity principle into absolute values that should guide all who care for children. In the tough words of the street: We won't "diss" our children or let others "diss" them either, and we won't let a youth "diss" anybody else, peers or staff. His organization conducts thorough "consumer evaluation" questions to ensure that children and families are treated with dignity. In periodic private interviews, evaluators ask students about the effectiveness, fairness, pleasantness, and concern of their staff. Says Father Peter: "We live in a society that routinely throws children away. That his or her caretakers might hurt a child is an outrage. It cries to heaven."[38]

The most direct evaluation is a measurement of the changes in individual students. It is beyond the scope of our discussion to examine the technical issues in assessing outcomes.[39] Often we have tested narrow outcomes but ignored the most important question: What is the measure of a successful life?

Albert Bandura has gathered decades of research showing that human well-being is tied to "self-efficacy."[40] In the Circle of Courage terms, this is Mastery and Independence. Young people need to meet difficult tasks as challenges. They need the skills to succeed, and the resilience to fail with courage. But Bandura warns that self-efficacy is a mixed blessing if it stands alone. Humans live in communities so they need to develop "collective efficacy." This translates to Belonging and Generosity in the Circle of Courage. James Kauffman observes that the spirit of generosity places high expectations on humans. This is more than giving things. True generosity requires enduring slights without retaliation. It requires a forgiving spirit and empathy.[41]

7. Leading by Serving

In *The Prophet*, Kahlil Gibran writes, "Work is love made visible." That ethic of service to others is the foundation of democratic communities and organizations. Leadership based on coercion and deception is incapable of developing courage, competence, and compassion in followers. Those who applaud the value of service-learning for students may not have considered that adults in authority should also model service to others. The servant-leadership principle applies not only to how administrators treat co-workers; it is equally relevant to any person, old or young, who is in a position to exercise leadership over others. Nancy Carlsson-Paige poses this question to educators: "How do I want to use my power with children? Everything a teacher does emanates from how this question gets answered."[42] In a culture that treats leaders as "superiors," joining leadership with servanthood may seem unappealing.

The concept of servant-leadership was developed by Robert Greenleaf and has been widely dispersed throughout the field of management. Greenleaf's writings on the connection between leadership and service deeply challenged entrenched notions of the boss manager. He noted that "service" is deeply rooted in religious traditions and is mentioned over 1,300 times in the Bible. Greenleaf was not a theologian but the director of management research at AT&T.[43]

Greenleaf attributes the idea that the best leader is a servant to the fictional writings of Hermann Hesse.[44] According to the story, a group of men set out on a journey. They were accompanied by Leo, who acted as servant and sustained them with his spirit and song. All went well until Leo disappeared and the group fell into total confusion. They couldn't even complete their journey without the servant. Later it was learned that Leo was a great and noble leader of the order that sponsored their journey.

Servant-leadership pushes the envelope in a culture that celebrates dominance. To clarify, servant-leadership is not a role reversal where followers give orders to their leader. As Ken Blanchard suggests, that would be like inmates running the prison.[45] Rather, the leader's task is to forge a community of co-workers where all join together pursuing a common goal. Stephen Covey concludes that servant-leadership is the most efficient management model possible. It empowers workers in high trust cultures and turns bosses into servants and coaches.

In contrast, dominating leadership is marked by adversarial relationships. One may boss subordinates but one cannot buy their hearts, minds, and spirits.[46]

The power of servant-leadership comes from the fact that true allegiance is only given to a respected and trusted leader. The leader supports the needs of those being served. The true test of service leadership is its effect on followers. Do they grow as persons? Do they work as a team? Do they become more competent, more autonomous, more likely to become servants themselves? The parallel with the Circle of Courage principles of belonging, mastery, independence, and generosity is clear.

The most inspiring stories in the human saga are leaders who serve with a generous spirit. Mother Teresa dedicated her life to the outcasts of India. Wu Fung sacrificed his own life to end the practice of human sacrifice in Taiwan. Gandhi, Martin Luther King, Jr., and Malcolm X died in the struggle for civil rights.

Perhaps the greatest example of servant-leadership on behalf of children is seen in the life of Dr. Janusz Korczak of Poland. He launched his career in 1901 with his book *Children of the Streets*. He founded a school for street children based on the premise that all children have the right to be respected. He invented systems of youth governance and advocated for youthful offenders before the court. He trained professionals and wrote twenty books on working with children. He started a national newspaper with 4,000 child-correspondents so the voice of youth could be heard. He gave advice to parents on a national radio show. But most of all, he lived for over 30 years in his orphanage, caring for Warsaw's Jewish street urchins.

When German troops occupied Poland, Korczak with his staff and 200 students were herded into the Warsaw Ghetto. Korczak penned the record of those final days in his *Ghetto Diary*.[47] He had been an avid reader of Rabindranath Tagore, the world-renowned poet who developed a school for cast-off children in Bolpur, India. When it became clear that the end was near, Korczak arranged for the children to perform *Post Office*, a story by Tagore about Amal, a dying Hindu boy. As the youngsters acted out the story, they were preparing for what was to come.

The troops arrived on an August day in 1942. The children, dressed in their best, left their residence marching in procession behind the tallest boy who carried a green flag emblazoned with the Star of David. The street was lined with onlookers as Dr. Korczak, his staff, and the children trudged to the train station. The occupying army did not want to create a martyr of this man who was a national treasure, so a high-ranking officer offered Dr. Korczak his freedom. He simply responded, "One does not leave one's child in sickness, in ill-fortune, or in danger."[48] Korczak and his children were loaded onto chlorinated boxcars bound for the gas chambers of Treblinka.

Korczak's diary was recovered after the war. His entries describe the daily struggle to teach and care for children in the face of the greatest adversity. Korczak also reflected on his lifetime of service to society's discarded youth. He wondered whether in 50 years the world might be civilized enough to respect the dignity of children. Still, he didn't consider his work a failure for he had been true to his vision. His final entry in the ghetto diary was simply: "I exist not to be loved but to love and to serve."

Works Cited

[1] Angelou. 2001.

[2] We gratefully acknowledge the assistance of John Kuenster, Executive Editor of Century Publishing Company, Evanston, IL, and co-author of *To Sleep with the Angels: The Story of a Fire*.

[3] Cowan and Kuenster. 1996.

[4] King, Jr. 1963.

[5] Ella Deloria was a Native American who grew up on a Lakota reservation in the 1890s. She was trained as an anthropologist and teacher at Columbia University. This citation is condensed from "A Better Way," which was her account of a murderer who was adopted by the aggrieved family. Brendtro, Brokenleg, and Van Bockern. 1990.

[6] Van Bockern, Kinsley, and Woodward. 2000.

174

[7] Braithwaite. 1989.

[8] Wilker. 1921/1993.

[9] Hibbler with Shahbazian. 2000.

[10] Benson. 1997.

[11] Ibid.

[12] This vision statement is from *In a New Light Initiative,* developed by schools, courts, and youth agencies in Calhoun County, MI, and chaired by Martin Mitchell.

[13] Garbarino and Eckenrode. 1997.

[14] Bavoleck. 2000.

[15] Harrison. 1993.

[16] Brendtro and Ness. 1983.

[17] Garfinkel. 1998.

[18] The Federation of Families for Children's Mental Health, phone 703-684-7710; www.ffcmh.org; Children and Adults with Attention Deficit Disorders [CHADD] telephone is 800-233-4050. www.chadd.org

[19] Richard Foster, Ed.D., began his teaching career in California schools in 1941. He was a principal in southern California schools and superintendent in Berkeley during the 1970s. As an expert on school leadership, he has helped school boards across the United States select superintendents and executives.

[20] Adapted from Richard Foster. 2000.

[21] Furstenberg, Cook, Eccles, Elder, and Sameroff. 1999.

[22] Heneggler, Schenwald, Borduin, Rowland, and Cunningham. 1998.

[23] Henggeler et. al. 1998. 132.

[24] Henggeler et. al. 1998. 130.

[25] Dishion, McCord, and Poulin. 1999.

[26] Gold and Osgood. 1992.

175

[27] Gibbs, Potter, and Goldstein. 1995.

[28] Lantieri. 2001.

[29] D. Myers, D. 2000.

[30] Larson and Brendtro. 2000.

[31] Peter. 1999.

[32] The Ministry Arts Program was developed by Ken Ponds, Chaplain, and Nobel Schuler, who directs Starr Commonwealth's arts programs.

[33] Don Barron, personal communication, Honolulu, HI, July 1973.

[34] Goldstein, 1997.

[35] Goldstein and Martens. 2000.

[36] Yang, Davis, Ryan and Wasmund. 1999.

[37] The Educational Environment Audit has been developed by the Starr Commonwealth Training and Resource Center, Albion, MI 49224. Telephone 517-629-5593.

[38] Peter. 1999.

[39] Breen and Fiedler. 1996.

[40] Bandura. 1995.

[41] Kauffman. 2000.

[42] Carlsson-Paige. 2001.

[43] Greenleaf. 1996.

[44] Hesse. 1992

[45] Blanchard. 1998.

[46] Covey. 1998.

[47] Korczak. 1979.

[48] Brendtro and Hinders. 1990.

Bibliography

Addams, Jane. 1909. *The spirit of youth and the city streets.* New York: MacMillan Company. 60–61.

Adler, Alfred. 1932. *Understanding human nature.* London: George Allen and Unwin, Ltd.

Aichhorn, August. 1935. *Wayward youth.* New York: Viking Press.

Alexander, P. 1994. *Alan Paton: A biography.* Oxford: Oxford University Press.

Ali, Hana. 2000. *Muhammad Ali's life lessons presented through his daughter's eyes.* New York: Pocket Books.

Allport, Gordon. 1958. *The nature of prejudice.* New York: Doubleday.

American Bar Association. 2000. *A gathering momentum: Continuing impacts of the American Bar Association's call for a moratorium on executions.* Washington, DC. Author.

America's prison generation. 2000. *Newsweek*, 13 November, 40–49.

Amnesty International. 1998. *Betraying the young: Human rights violations against children in the U.S. justice system.* AI Index: AMR 51/57/98. New York: Amnesty International USA.

Amnesty International. 1998. *On the wrong side of history: Children and the death penalty in the USA.* New York: Amnesty International USA.

Angelou, Maya. 2001. Cited by Jane Ammeson, Maya Angelou uncaged. *World Traveler.* May, 38–43.

Anglin, James. 1992. Children's rights and the magic beanstalk. *Journal of Emotional and Behavioral Problems, 1*(3):36–39.

Ashe, Arthur, and Arnold Rampersad. 1993. *Days of grace*. New York: Alfred A. Knopf.

Athens, Lonnie H. 1992. *The creation of dangerous violent criminals*. Urbana, IL: University of Illinois Press.

Baker, S., and R. Gersten. 2000. *Balancing qualitative/quantitative research*. Paper presented to OSEP Research Project Director's Conference, Washington, D.C., 14 July.

Bandura, Albert. 1982. The psychology of chance encounters and life paths. *American Psychologist*, 27(7):47–55.

Bandura, Albert, ed. 1995. *Self efficacy in changing societies*. Cambridge, UK: Cambridge University Press.

Bandura, A., C. Barbaranelli, G.V. Caprara, and C. Pastorelli. 1996. Mechanisms of moral disengagement in the exercise of moral agency. *Journal of Personality and Social Psychology*, 71:364–374.

Barnao, Peter. 1999. Boy rapist sent to adult court. *The Dominion*. Wellington, New Zealand, 6 August, 1.

Bavoleck. Steven. J. 2000. The nurturing parenting programs. *Juvenile Justice Bulletin*. Washington, D.C.: OJJDP. November.

Beck, Aaron. 1999. *Prisoners of hate: The cognitive basis of anger, hostility, and violence*. New York: Harper Collins.

Benedict, Ruth. 1938. Continuities and discontinuities in cultural conditioning. *Psychiatry*, 1:161–167.

Benson, Peter L. 1997. *All kids are our kids: What communities must do to raise caring and responsible children and adolescents*. San Francisco: Jossey-Bass.

Berkey, L. G., B. J. Keyes, and J. E. Longhurst. 2001. "Bully-proofing: What One District Learned About Improving School Climate." *Reclaiming Children and Youth*, 9(4):224–228.

B'Hahn, Carmella. 2001. Be the change you want to see: An interview with Arun Gandhi." *Reclaiming Children and Youth*, 10(1):6–9.

Bishop, D., C. Frasier, L. Lonza-Kaduce, and L. Winner. 1996. The transfer of juveniles to criminal court: Does it make a difference? *Crime and Delinquency*, April, 422:171–191.

Blanchard, Kenneth. 1998. Servant-leadership revisited. In *Insights in leadership*, ed. Larry C. Spears, 15–20. New York: John Wiley and Sons, Inc..

Bower, Eli M. 1960. *Early identification of emotionally handicapped children in school*. Springfield, IL: Charles C. Thomas.

Boyd, L. M. 1999. Youthful St. Francis was in a gang. *Traverse City* (Michigan) *Record Eagle*. 8 November, 4C.

Braithwaite, John. 1989. *Crime, shame, and reintegration*. Cambridge, UK: Cambridge University Press.

Breen, Michael. J., and Craig B. Fiedler, eds. 1996. *Behavioral approach to assessment of youth with emotional/behavioral disorders: A handbook for school-based practitioners*. Austin, TX: Pro-ED.

Brendtro, L. 1965. *Verbal and conceptual factors in preadolescent boys with impaired relationship capacity*. Doctoral Dissertation. Ann Arbor, MI: University of Michigan.

Brendtro, Larry. 1986. Philosophy and practices of service learning." *Child Care Quarterly*, 14(1).

Brendtro, Larry. 1995. Furious kids and treatment myths. *Journal of Emotional and Behavioral Problems*, 3(2):8–12.

Brendtro, Larry. 1998. Synergistic relationships: The powerful 'SR' of re-education. *Residential Treatment for Children & Youth*, 15(3):25–35.

Brendtro, L., and J. Bacon. 1995. Youth Empowerment and Teamwork. In *Teamwork models and experience in education,* ed. H. Garner, 55–72. Boston: Allyn and Bacon.

Brendtro, Larry, and Joan Bacon. 1992. *Teamwork in programs for children and youth: A handbook for administrators,* ed. H. Garner. Springfield, IL: Charles C. Thomas Publishers.

Brendtro, Larry, Martin Brokenleg, and Steve Van Bockern. 1990. *Reclaiming youth at risk: Our hope for the future.* Bloomington, IN: National Educational Service.

Brendtro, Larry, and James Cunningham. 1998. Meeting the developmental needs of incarcerated youth. *Reclaiming Children and Youth,* 7(2):104–109.

Brendtro, Larry, and Denise Hinders. 1990. A saga of Janusz Korczak, the king of children. *Harvard Educational Review,* 60(2):237–246.

Brendtro, L., and N. J. Long. 1995. Reclaiming violent students. *Educational Leadership,* 52(5):52–56.

Brendtro, Larry, and Martin Mitchell. 1983. The organizational ethos: From tension to teamwork. In L. K. Brendtro and A. E. Ness, *Re-educating troubled youth: Powerful environments for teaching and treatment,* 94–122. Chicago: Aldine.

Brendtro, Larry, and Arlin Ness. 1982. Perspectives on peer group treatment: The use and abuse of guided group interaction/positive peer culture." *Children and Youth Services Review,* 4(4):307–324.

Brendtro, Larry, and Arlin Ness. 1983. *Re-educating troubled youth.* New York: Aldine de Gruyter.

Brendtro, Larry, and Arlin Ness. 1995. Counterfeit conservatism and the war on crime. *Reclaiming Children and Youth,* 4(1):18–24.

Bridgeland, M. 1971. *Pioneer work with maladjusted children.* London: Staples Press.

Bronfenbrenner, Urie. 1979. *The ecology of human development*. Cambridge, MA: Harvard University Press.

Brown, Waln. 1983. *The other side of delinquency*. New Brunswick, NJ: Rutgers University Press.

Brown, Waln. 1988. The post intervention experience: A self-report examination of deviancy devolution. In *The abandonment of delinquent behavior*, eds. R. L. Jenkins and W. K. Brown, 42–55. New York: Praeger.

Buber, Martin. 1970. *I and Thou*. New York: Charles Scribner and Sons.

Burns, David. 1993. *Ten days to self-esteem*. New York: St. Martins.

Bush, Bill. 2001. Columbus schools get failing grade in dropout study. *Columbus* [Ohio] *Dispatch*. 23 January, A1–2.

Calhoun, John. 1998. My brother's keeper. *Reclaiming Children and Youth*, 7(2):74–76.

Cambone, Joseph. 1994. *Teaching troubled children: A case study in effective classroom practice*. New York: Teachers College Press.

Carlsson-Paige, Nancy. 2001. Nurturing meaningful connections with young children. In *Schools with spirit: Nurturing the inner lives of children and teachers*, ed. Linda Lantieri, 21–38. Boston: Beacon Press.

CBS. 2001. A three year nightmare. *Sixty Minutes II*. New York: CBS. 2 January.

Chambers, Jamie C. 2001. Keynote address, Youth Off the Streets Conference, Sydney, Australia, 23 May 2001.

Chambers, Jamie C. 2000. Unmasking the terror. *Reclaiming Children and Youth*, 9(1):14–17.

Confucius. In Waley, Arthur. 1938. *The analects of Confucius*. New York: Random House. Cited by Shin Sook Kang. 1991. *Confucius: His philosophy in teaching*. Unpublished Manuscript. Sioux Falls, SD: Augustana College. 9.

Cook, John, ed. 1996. *The book of positive quotations*. Minneapolis, MN: Fairview.

Cooper, Desiree. 1999. Stolen childhood. *Detroit* (Michigan) *Free Press*. 8 November, B1, 4.

Cothern, Lynn. 2000. *Juveniles and the death penalty*. Washington, D.C.: U.S. Department of Justice, Coordinating Council on Juvenile Justice and Delinquency Prevention.

Covey, Stephen R. 1998. Servant-leadership from the inside out. *Insights in leadership*, ed. Larry C. Spears. New York: John Wiley and Sons, Inc.

Cowan, David, and John Kuenster. 1996. *To sleep with the angels: The story of a fire*. Chicago: Ivan R. Dee.

Dishion, T. J., J. McCord, and F. Poulin. 1999. When interventions harm: Peer groups and problem behavior. *American Psychologist, 54*(9):755–784.

Docherty, J. P. 2000. Presentation at Brown Schools. Sandpoint, ID. 19 April.

Dodge, K. A., J. E. Lochman, J. D. Harnish, J. E. Bates, and G. S. Petit. 1997. Reactive and proactive aggression in school children and psychiatrically impaired and chronically assaultive youth. *Journal of Abnormal Psychology, 106*:37–51.

Dryfoos, Joy G. 1994. *Full-service schools*. San Francisco: Jossey-Bass.

Durkheim, Emile. 1972. In *Emile Durkheim: Selected writings*, ed. Anthony Giddens. Cambridge, U.K.: Cambridge University Press.

Edwards, Rose. 1994. Makarenko's road to life. *Journal of Emotional and Behavioral Problems,* 3(1):56–59.

Epstein, Michael. 1998. Assessing the emotional and behavioral strengths of children. *Reclaiming Children and Youth,* 6(4):250–252.

Fahlberg, Vera. 1991. *A child's journey through placement.* Indianapolis, IN: Perspectives Press.

Feld, Barry. 1999. *Bad kids: Race and the transformation of the juvenile court.* New York: Oxford University Press.

Fine, Michelle. 1993. Making controversy: Who's at risk? In *Children at risk in America,* ed. Roberta Wollons, 91–110. Albany, NY: Albany State University Press.

Fitzpatrick, T. 1978. The angels fire confession. *Chicago Sun Times.* 3 December, A8–9.

Foster, Herbert L. 1986. *Ribbin', jivin', and playin' the dozens: The persistent dilemma in our schools.* Cambridge, MA: Ballinger Publishing Company.

Foster, Richard. 2000. Face to face with our future. *Reclaiming Children and Youth,* 8(4): 200–202.

Friends of the Orphans. 2000. From material presented by Friends of the Orphans, Tempe, AZ, to Kellogg's Hannah Neil World of Children Award. Columbus, Ohio, 10 May, 2000.

Furstenberg, F., T. Cook, J. Eccles, G. Elder, and A. Sameroff. 1999. *Managing to make it: Urban families and adolescent success.* Chicago: University of Chicago Press.

Gabor, Peter, and I. Greene. 1991. Views from the inside: Young people's perceptions of residential services. *Journal of Child and Youth Care Work,* 7:6–19.

Garbarino, J., and J. Eckenrode. 1997. *Understanding abusive families: An ecological approach to theory and practice.* San Francisco: Jossey-Bass.

Garfinkel, Lilly. 1998. Children with disabilities in the justice system. *Reclaiming Children and Youth,* 7(2):80–82.

Garmezy, Norman. 1994. In R. J. Haggerty, L. Sherrod, Norman Garmezy, and M. Rutter. *Stress, risk, and resilience in children and adolescents.* New York: Cambridge.

Garner, Howard. 1982. *Teamwork in programs for children and youth: A handbook for administrators.* Springfield, IL: Charles C. Thomas Publishers.

Garrity, Carla, Kathryn Jens, William Porter, Nancy Sager, and Cam Short-Camilli. 2000. *Bully-proofing your elementary school.* Longmont, CO: Sopris West.

Gibbs, John, Granville Potter, and Arnold Goldstein. 1995. *The EQUIP Program: Teaching youth to think and act responsibly through a peer-helping approach.* Champaign, IL: Research Press.

Gibbs, John, Granville Potter, Arnold Goldstein, and Larry Brendtro. 1996. From harassment to helping with antisocial youth. *Reclaiming Children and Youth,* 5(1):40–46.

Gibbs, John, Granville Potter, Arnold Goldstein, and Larry Brendtro. 1998. How EQUIP programs help youth change. *Reclaiming Children and Youth,* 7(2):117–122.

Gilliam, Bobby, Ashley Nicholas, and Debbie Saap. 2000. From guns to generosity. *Reclaiming Children and Youth,* 8(4):246–248.

Gilligan, C. 1982. *In a different voice.* Cambridge, MA: Harvard University Press.

Gilligan, James. 1997. *Violence: Reflections on a national epidemic.* New York: Random House.

Gillogly, Robert. 1993. The power of prevention: Dr. Karl Menninger. *Journal of Emotional and Behavioral Problems,* 1(4):44–47.

Glueck, Sheldon, and Eleanor Glueck. 1957. Cited in Leo
Kanner, *Child Psychiatry*, (3rd Ed.). Springfield, IL: Charles
C. Thomas.

Gold, M. 1995. Charting a course: promise and prospects for
alternative schools. *Journal of Emotional and Behavioral
Disorders*, 3(4):8–11.

Gold, Martin, and D. W. Osgood. 1992. *Personality and peer
influence in juvenile correction*. Westport, CT: Greenwood
Press.

Goldstein, Arnold. 1991. *Delinquent gangs*. Champaign, IL:
Research Press.

Goldstein, Arnold. 1997. Controlling vandalism. In A. Goldstein
and J. Conoley, *School violence intervention: A practical
handbook*, 290–320. New York: Guilford Publications.

Goldstein, Arnold P. 1999a. *Low level aggression: First steps on
the ladder to violence*. Champaign, IL: Research Press.

Goldstein, Arnold P. 1999b. Aggression reduction strategies:
Effective and ineffective. *School Psychology Quarterly*,
14(1):40–58.

Goldstein, Arnold, K. Heller, and L. Sechrest. 1966.
Psychotherapy and the psychology of behavior change. New
York: John Wiley & Sons, Inc.

Goldstein, Arnold P., and B. K. Martens. 2000. *Lasting change:
Methods for enhancing generalization of gain*. Champaign,
IL: Research Press.

Goodlad, John, R. Soder, and K. Sirotnik, eds. 1993. *The moral
dimensions of teaching*. San Francisco: Jossey-Bass.

Gordon, Diane. 1990. *The justice juggernaut*. New Brunswick,
NJ: Rutgers University Press.

Greenleaf, Robert K. 1996. *On becoming a servant leader*. San
Francisco: Jossey-Bass.

Guthrie, Doug, and Theresa McClellan. 2000. Backgrounds of the accused. *Grand Rapids* (Michigan) *Press.* 29 October, A23.

Haggerty, Robert J., and Norman Garmezy. 1994. In Robert J. Haggerty, Lonnie Sherrod, Norman Garmezy, and Michael Rutter. *Stress, risk, and resilience in children and adolescents.* New York: Cambridge.

Hale, R. L. 1997. *A review of juvenile executions in America. Criminology Series, Volume 3.* Lewiston, NY: Edwin Mellen Press.

Hall, Samuel. 1829. *Lectures on school-keeping.* Boston: Richardson, Lord and Holbrook.

Harkins, S. 1991. *The IEP as a lived experience: Portraits of students in behavior disorder programs.* Doctoral Dissertation, National College of Education, National-Louis University, Chicago.

Harris, J. R. 1998. *The nurture assumption: Why children turn out the way they do.* New York: Free Press.

Harrison, Margaret. 1993. Hooray! Here comes Tuesday! *Journal of Emotional and Behavioral Problems,* 2(4):58–60.

Hawkins. 1994. In Robert J. Haggerty, Lonnie Sherrod, Norman Garmezy, and Michael Rutter. *Stress, risk, and resilience in children and adolescents.* New York: Cambridge.

Healy, W., and A. F. Bronner. 1936. *New light on delinquency and its treatment: Results of a research conducted for the Institute of human relations.* New Haven, CT: Yale University Press.

Heilbrun, A. and M. Heilbrun. 1985. Psychopathy and dangerousness. *British Journal of Clinical Psychology,* 24:181–195.

Heneggler, S., S. Schenwald, C. Borduin, M. Rowland, and P. Cunningham. 1998. *Multisystemic Treatment of Antisocial Behavior in Children and Adolescents.* New York: Guilford Press.

Hesse, Herman. 1992. *The journey to the east*. New York: The Noonday Press.

Hewitt, J. J. 1998. *The myth of self esteem*. New York: St. Martins.

Hibbler, William. J. with Mary Shahbazian. 2000. We cannot afford to fail them: A dialogue with the presiding judge of the world's first juvenile court. *Reclaiming Children and Youth*, 8(3):145–150.

His Law, Jerome. 1993. Treat me with respect. *Journal of Emotional and Behavioral Problems*, 1(4):93.

Hobbs, Nicholas. 1994. *The troubled and troubling child*. Columbus, OH: AREA.

Hoover, John, and Glenn Olson. 2000. Sticks and stones may break their bones: Teasing as bullying. *Reclaiming Children and Youth*, 9(2):87–91.

Hyman, Irwin A. 1997. *School discipline and school violence*. Boston: Allyn and Bacon.

Hyman, Irwin. A. 2000. *Dangerous schools/dangerous students: Defining and assessing student alienation syndrome*. OSEP Research Project Director's Conference, 13 July. Washington, D.C.

Ivanoff, Andre, Betty J. Blythe, and Tony Tripodi. 1994. *Involuntary clients in social work practice: A research-based approach*. New York: Aldine de Gruyter.

Jones, M., and B. Krisberg. 1994. *Juvenile crime. Youth violence and public policy*. San Francisco: National Council on Crime and Delinquency.

Kanner, Leo. 1957. *Child psychiatry*, (3rd Ed.). Springfield, IL: Charles C. Thomas.

Katz, Fred. A. 1993. *Ordinary people and extraordinary evil*. Albany: State University of New York Press.

Kauffman, J. 1994. Violent children and youth: A call for action. *Journal of Emotional and Behavioral Problems,* 3(1):25–26.

Kauffman, James. 2000. Future directions with troubled children. *Reclaiming Children and Youth,* 9(2):119–124.

Kazdin, Alfred E. 1994. Interventions for aggressive and antisocial children. In *Reason to hope: A psychosocial perspective on youth violence,* eds. L. Roon, J. Gentry, and P. Schlegel, 341–392. Washington, D.C.: American Psychological Association.

Kellerman, Jonathan. 1999. *Savage spawn: Reflections on violent children.* New York: Ballantine.

Kilpatrick, W., ed. 1951. Pestalozzi: *The education of man.* New York: Philosophical Library.

King, Martin Luther. 1963. *Strength to love.* Philadelphia: Fortress.

Kipnis, Aaron. 1999. *Angry young men: How parents, teachers and counselors can help bad boys become good men.* San Francisco: Jossey-Bass.

Kirkland, Jack A. 2000. Straight talk about racism. *Reclaiming Children and Youth,* (1):9–13.

Kivel, P. 1996. *Uprooting racism.* Gabriola Island, BC: New Society Publishers.

Knitzer, J., Z. Steinberg, and B. Fleisch. 1990. *At the schoolhouse door.* New York: Bank Street College of Education.

Korczak, Janus. 1929. The child's right to respect. Reprinted in J. Korczak (1967). *Selected works of Janusz Korczak,* ed. M. Wolins, trans. J. Bachrach, 463–500. Warsaw, Poland: National Science Foundation.

Korczak, Janus. 1967. *Janusz Korczak: Collected works.* Warsaw: United Nations.

Korczak, Janus. 1979. *Ghetto Diary*. Washington, D.C.: University Press of America.

Kress, Catherine, and Nancy Forrest. 2000. The VOICES project. *Reclaiming Children and Youth,* 9(2):116–119.

Krisberg, B., and J. Austin. 1993. *Reinventing juvenile justice*. Newbury Park, CA: Sage Publications.

Lantieri, Linda. 2001. *Schools with spirit*. Boston: Beacon Press.

Lantieri, Linda. 2001. An ounce of prevention is worth a pound of metal detectors. *Reclaiming Children and Youth, 10*(1): 36–41.

Lantieri, Linda, and Janet Patti. 1996. *Waging peace in our schools*. Boston: Beacon Press

Larson, Reed. 2000. Toward a psychology of positive youth development. *American Psychologist, 55*(1):170–183.

Larson, Scott, and Larry Brendtro. 2000. *Reclaiming our prodigal sons and daughters*. Bloomington, IN: National Educational Service.

Laursen, Eric. 2000. Strength-based practice with children in trouble. *Reclaiming Children and Youth,* 9(2):70–75.

Levy, Zvi. 1993. *Negotiating positive identity in a group care community: Reclaiming uprooted youth*. New York: Haworth Press.

Lewis, D. O., et al. 1988. Neuropsychiatric, psychoeducational, and family characteristics of 14 juveniles condemned to death in the United States. *American Journal of Psychiatry, 145*(5):585–589.

Liepmann, C. M. 1928. Die Selbstventaltung der Grefangenen. In Liepmann, M. (ed), *Hamburgishe Schriftn zur Gesamten Strafrechstswessenschaft (Vol. 12)*. Berlin: Mannheim.

Listen to Us! 1978. New York: Workman Publishing.

Loeber, R., and D. P. Farrington, eds. 1999. *Serious & violent juvenile offenders: Risk factors and successful interventions.* Thousand Oaks, CA: Sage Publications.

Long, Nicholas. 1994. Inclusion: Formula for failure? *Journal of Emotional and Behavioral Problems,* 3(1):19–23.

Long, Nicholas, Frank Fecser, and Larry Brendtro. 1998. Life space crisis intervention: New skills for reclaiming students showing patterns of self-defeating behavior. *Healing,* 3(2):2–21.

Long, Nicholas, Frank Fecser, and Mary Wood. 2001. *Life space crisis intervention.* Austin, TX: Pro-Ed.

Males, Michael A. 1996. *The scapegoat generation: America's war on adolescents.* Monroe, ME: Common Courage Press.

Marquand, Robert. 2001. Chinese teachers warned of 40 forbidden phrases. *National Post-Canada.* 4 May, A9.

Marquoit, James and Martha Dobbins. 1998. Strength-based treatment for juvenile sexual offenders. *Reclaiming Children and Youth,* 7(1):40–43.

Martinson, R. 1974. What works? Questions and answers about prison reform. *The Public Interest,* 35:25.

McBride, M. 1979. *The fire that will not die.* Palm Springs, CA: ETC Publications.

McCall, Herman J. 1996. *Factors that relate to the drop-out rate of students that successfully complete an alternative education program.* Doctoral Dissertation, California Coast University.

Meade, George H. 1918. The psychology of punitive justice. *The American Journal of Sociology XXIII*:577–602.

Mendler, Alan, and Richard Curwin. 1999. *Discipline with dignity for challenging youth.* Bloomington, IN: National Education Service.

Menninger, Karl. 1966. *The crime of punishment*. New York: Viking Press.

Meyers, D. 2000. The funds, friends, and faith of happy people. *American Psychologist*, 55(1):56–57.

Mitchell, M. 1982. *The relationship of treatment team interpersonal communication to staff-to-client relationships in a residential treatment setting*. Doctoral Dissertation. Kalamazoo, MI: Western Michigan University.

Mitchell, Martin, and Christine Ameen. 1985. Administrative styles and teamwork. In *Teamwork models and experience in education*, ed. H. Garner, 125–138. Boston: Allyn and Bacon.

Mitchell, Martin, Christi Tobin Barrett, and John Seita. 1998. *Connectedness, continuity, dignity & opportunity: Principle-based action for kids*. Albion, MI: Starr Commonwealth.

Montague, Ashley. 1978. *Touching: The human significance of the skin*. New York: Harper and Row.

Morgan, John J. B. 1936. *The psychology of the unadjusted school child*. New York: Macmillan.

Montessori, Maria. 1967, 1995. *The Absorbent Mind*. New York: Henry Holt and Company.

Morrison, Blake. 2000. A fatal mystery shrouds flight 1763. *USA Today*. Arlington, VA. 18 December, 1A.

Murray-Seegert, Carola. 1989. *Nasty girls, thugs, and humans like us*. Baltimore, MD: Paul H. Brookes.

Murray, Eric. 1999. Experts disagree on usefulness of 'the box' for impaired students. *Marshall* (Michigan) *Chronicle*. 12 February.

Myers, D. 2000. The funds, friends, and faith of happy people. *American Psychologist*, 55(1):56–67.

Nelson, G. E., and R. W. Lewak. 1988. Delinquency and attachment. In R. L. Jenkins and W. K. Brown. *The abandonment of delinquent behavior: Promoting the turnaround.* New York: Praeger.

Ness, C. 2000. *Emotional expressiveness and problematic behaviors among male juvenile sexual offenders, general offenders, and nonoffenders.* Doctoral Dissertation. Kalamazoo, MI: Western Michigan University.

Newkirk, Reginald, and Nathan Rutstein. 2000. *Racial healing: The institutes for the healing of racism.* Albion, MI: National Resource Center for the Healing of Racism.

Nichols, Polly. 1996. Lessons on lookism. *Reclaiming Children and Youth,* 5(2):118–122.

Nichols, Polly and Martha Shaw. 1999. *Whispering shadows: Think clearly & claim your personal power.* Iowa City, IA: River Lights.

Odney, John R., and Larry K. Brendtro. 1992. Students grade their schools. *Journal of Emotional and Behavioral Problems,* 2(1):4–9.

Olive, Edna. 1999. 'I was completely out of control': Kevin takes charge of his life. *Reclaiming Children and Youth,* 8(1):7–11.

Olweus, Dan. 1978. *Aggression in the schools: Bullies and whipping boys.* New York: Wiley.

Parese, S. 1999. Understanding the impact of personal crisis on school performance in troubled youth. *Reclaiming Children and Youth,* 8(3):181–187.

Parks, Alexia. 2000. *An American gulag: Secret P.O.W. camps for teens.* Eldorado, CO: The Education Exchange Network.

Paton, Alan. 1948. *Cry, the beloved country.* New York: Scribner.

Paton, Alan. 1986. *Diepkloof: Reflections of Diepkloof Reformatory*. Capetown, South Africa: Credo Press. 103.

Perlman, H. 1979. *Relationships: The heart of helping people*. Chicago: University of Chicago Press.

Peter, Val. 1999. *What makes Boys Town succeed*. Boys Town, NE: Boys Town Press.

Petit, Michael, and Thomas R. Brooks. 1998. Abuse and delinquency: Two sides of the same coin. *Reclaiming Children and Youth,* 7(2):77–79.

Pipher, Mary. 1996. When girls become bullies." *Reclaiming Children and Youth,* 5(1):34.

Quirk, Constance, and Mary Wood. 1999. Protection from the badness of the world." *Reclaiming Children and Youth,* 8(1):50–55.

Ramsey, G. V. 1943. The sexual development of boys. *American Journal of Psychiatry,* 56(3):217–234.

Raychaba, Brian. 1992. Voices of youth: Doing and being done to. *Journal of Emotional and Behavioral Problems,* 1(3):4–9.

Redl, F., and D. Wineman. 1951. *Children who hate*. New York: The Free Press.

Reese, Charley. 1998. How to make America safe. *The Herald-Mail.* 6 June, A4. Hagerstown, MD.

Regnery, Alfred. 1986. A federal perspective on juvenile justice reform. *Crime and Delinquency,* 32(1):39–52.

Reinharz, P. 1996. *Killer kids, bad law: Tales of the juvenile court system*. New York: Barricade Books.

Rhode, Ginger, William R. Jensen, and H. Kenton Reavis. 1996. *The tough kid book: Practical classroom management strategies*. Longmont, CO: Sopris West.

193

Riak, Jordan. 2001. *Boot camp for kids: Torturing teenagers for fun and profit.* http://nospank.org/boot.htm. Printed 1/6/01.

Rutstein, Nathan. 2000. Frontiers in healing racism. *Reclaiming Children and Youth,* 9(1) 29–35.

Sadker, Myra, and David Sadker. 1994. *Failing at fairness: How America's schools cheat girls.* New York: Charles Scribner's Sons.

Safran, J. D., and J. C. Muran. 2000. *Negotiating the therapeutic alliance: A relational treatment guide.* New York: Guilford Press.

Sanders, Wiley B., ed. 1970. *Juvenile offenders for a thousand years.* Chapel Hill, NC. University of North Carolina Press.

Saurman, K., and R. Nash. 1980. An antidote to narcissism. *Synergist,* 9(1): 16–18.

Schwartz, Ira M., and Gideon Fishman. 1999. *Kids raised by the government.* Westport, CT: Praeger.

Seita, John, Martin Mitchell, and Christi Tobin. 1996. *In whose best interest? One child's odyssey, a nation's responsibility.* Elizabethtown, PA: Continental Press.

Seita, John, and Larry Brendtro. 2001. *Kids who outwit adults.* Longmont, CO: Sopris West.

Seligman, M., and M. Csikszentmihalyi. 2000. Positive psychology: an introduction. *American Psychologist,* 55(1):5–14.

Selye, Hans. 1978. *The stress of life* (Rev. Ed.). New York: McGraw Hill.

Sherman, L. W. 1993. Defiance, deterrence, and irrelevance: A theory of the criminal sanction. *Journal of Research in Crime and Delinquency,* 30(4):445–477.

Simon, Peter. 2000. Tempest in a t-shirt: Controversial method of punishment divides brockton district. *Buffalo* (New York) *News.* 5 March, C1, 4.

Skinner, B. F. 1989. *Recent issues in the analysis of behavior.* Columbus, OH: Merrill.

Sprick, Randy, Mickey Garrison, and Lisa Howard. 1998. *CHAMPs: A proactive and positive approach to classroom management.* Longmont, CO: Sopris West.

Starr, Floyd. 1915. Bad boy? No such animal. *The Chicago Daily News.* 8 October.

Steinberg, Zina. 1994. 'Dare I disturb the universe?' Teaching, learning and the relational matrix." *Journal of Emotional and Behavioral Problems, 3*(1):11–14.

Stuart, J. 1997. *The young offender with disabilities.* Pacer Center Juvenile Justice Project. National Training of Trainers Institute. Minneapolis, MN. 4 September.

Trieschman, Al, James Whittaker, and Larry Brendtro. 1967. *The other 23 hours.* Chicago: Aldine.

Tully, Fred, and Larry Brendtro. 1998. Reaching angry and unattached kids. *Reclaiming Children and Youth, 7*(3): 147–154.

Tyler, T. R. 1990. *Why people obey the law.* New Haven, CT: Yale University.

Van Bockern, Steve, Paul Kinsley, Jon Woodward. 2000. To punish or to heal? Real justice in school and community. *Reclaiming Children and Youth, 8*(4):242–245.

Varenhorst, Barbara. 1984. Peer counseling: Past promises, current status and future directions. In *Handbook of counseling psychology,* 716–751. New York: Wiley.

Vilakazi, H. 1993. Rediscovering lost truths. *Journal of Emotional and Behavioral Problems, 1*(4):37.

Vorrath, H., and Larry Brendtro. 1974. *Positive peer culture.* Chicago: Aldine Publishing Company.

196

Vorrath, H., and Larry Brendtro. 1985. *Positive peer culture,* (2nd Ed.). New York: Aldine de Gruyter.

Walker, Hill, G. Colvin, and E. Ramsey 1995. *Antisocial behavior in school: Strategies and best practices.* New York: Books Cole.

Walker, Hill M., and Herbert H. Severson. 1992. *Systematic screening for behavior disorders.* Longmont, CO: Sopris West.

Walsh, Anthony, and J. Arthur Beyer. 1987. Violent delinquency and examination of psychopathic typologies. *Journal of Genetic Psychology, 148*(3):358–392.

Wasmund, William C. and Thomas F. Tate. 1995. *Partners in empowerment.* Albion, MI: Starr Commonwealth.

Werner, Emmy, and Ruth Smith. 1992. *Overcoming the odds: High risk children from birth to adulthood.* Ithaca, NY: Cornell University Press.

Whitt, Joseph C., Edward J. Daly, and George H. Noell. 2000. *Functional assessments: A step-by-step guide to solving academic & behavioral problems.* Longmont, CO: Sopris West.

Wickman, E. K. 1928. *Children's behavior and teachers' attitudes.* New York: The Commonwealth Fund.

Wilker, Karl. 1921/1993. *Der Lindenhof.* Heilbronnam Neckar: Lichtkampf-Verlag Nanns Altermann. Translated in 1993 by Stephen Lhotsky. Published by Augustana College, Sioux Falls, SD.

Wilson, J., and R. Herrnstine. 1985. *Crime and human nature.* New York: Simon and Schuster. 282–283, 297.

Wolin, Sybil, and Steven J. Wolin. 2000. Shifting paradigms: Easier said than done. *Strength Based Services International Newsletter,* 1–4.

Wolin, Steven J. and Sybil Wolin. 1993. *The resilient self: How survivors of troubled families rise above adversity.* New York: Villard.

Wood, Frank. 1995. Positive responses to student resistance to programs of behavior change. *Reclaiming Children and Youth,* 4(1):30–33.

Wood, Mary, Larry Brendtro, Frank Fecser, and Polly Nichols. 1999. *Psychoeducation, an idea whose time has come.* Reston, VA: Council for Children with Behavioral Disorders.

Woodward, John. 1999. *Reclaiming gang involved youth through sports.* Masters Thesis. Sioux Falls, SD: Augustana College Graduate School.

Wylie, Mary S. 1998. Public enemies. *Family Therapy Networker,* 22(3):24–37.

Yang, Huilan, Randy Davis, Joseph Ryan, and William Wasmund. 1999. *Assessing the climate of residential programs: Development and application of youth environmental survey.* Albion, MI: Starr Commonwealth.

Other Publications of Interest from Sopris West

Kids Who Outwit Adults

by John R. Seita, Ed.D. and Larry K. Brendtro, Ph.D.

Grades K–12

Strength-Based Interventions for Your Toughest Kids
—From Starr Commonwealth

In *Kids Who Outwit Adults*, authors Seita and Brendtro disclose the "private logic" behind kids' violent and defiant acts. Weaving together an effective, highly rewarding approach based on tried-and-true resilience models, insights from their years of experience working with youths, and youths' own heart wrenching accounts, the authors illuminate the *internal strengths and external supports* kids need in order to break out of these negative behavior patterns. Seita and Brendtro are your guides through the deeper world of youth scare tactics and coping mechanisms.

Product code: 160OUT

Powerful Struggles: Managing Resistance, Building Rapport

by John Maag, Ph.D.

Grades: K–12

John Maag offers novel approaches to teachers dealing with challenging student behaviors, showing how you can achieve dramatic, positive results by refocusing on your own behavior. Instead of continuing to use the same old methods without success, you'll learn how to respond in new ways that really work.

With this in-depth exploration of the nature of resistance, illustrated by real-life examples of the strategies in practice, you will discover the secrets of turning resistance into compliance including:

- Which strategy to choose, how to test it, and when to stop and try another
- How to eliminate challenging behaviors—and replace them with appropriate ones
- Three proven techniques for building rapport
- Three powerful methods for keeping your emotions in line—even in the most confrontational situations
- The most effective methods for building momentum in your classroom, and more.

Product code: 149RESIST

The Acting-Out Child
Coping with Classroom Disruption
by Hill M. Walker, Ph.D.

Grades K–6

Gain a thorough understanding of acting-out behavior—its origins and development, why common attempts to cope with inappropriate behavior fail, which strategies really do work, how to assess behavior, how best to combine interventions, how to defuse oppositional and aggressive behavior, and more. This comprehensive second edition of the Walker classic provides case studies, model interventions, and suggestions for how to reintegrate acting-out students into general education classrooms.

Product code: 55ACTING

To order these products, or for more information,
contact Sopris West at **(800) 547-6747**
or visit our website: **www.sopriswest.com**.

SOPRIS
WEST